Germany and

1000 Years of Shared History

Deutschland und Irland

1000 Jahre gemeinsamer Geschichte

Martin Elsasser

BROOKSIDE

Germany and Ireland / Deutschland und Irland

First published 1997

reprinted 1998

by

Brookside

2 Brookside

Dundrum Rd

Dundrum

Dublin 14

Text © Martin Elsasser 1997

The author has asserted his moral rights

ISBN: 1 873748 04 3

Cover design: Jon Berkeley

The Saints Kilian, Kolonat and Totnan. Inspired by the Hirsau Passionale (between 1125 and 1150) - Württembergische Landesbibliothek Stuttgart

Typesetting and printing:

e-print Ltd., Dublin.

Contents / Inhaltsverzeichnis

Germany and Ireland

1000 Years of Shared History

Martin Elsasser

This bool

German fi

and influen

The read

formed less

contributions

This book

spare its read   _ in-

numerable mon   . practically every aspect

of Irish-German r .....ons.

Readers seeking a more in-depth study of individual themes will find a select bibliography at the end of the book.

I wish to thank my friend Daragh Downes, B.A. for his revision of the English version of this book.

Martin Elsasser, Dublin, June 1997

1. Celtic Ancestors, Irish Saints

Our common history starts with the Celts. Not only the Irish, the Germans too share Celtic roots: large parts of what are now Germany, Austria and the Czech Republic (Bohemia) were inhabited by Celtic tribes. It was only during what is known as the 'migration of the peoples' from the fourth to the sixth century A.D. that these Celts were either absorbed or pushed into smaller enclaves (mostly less fertile mountain regions) by Germanic tribes. In the course of time they lost their Celtic identity.

Many archaeological finds bear witness to the high level of development of the Celts in the now German speaking area. They belong to what are known as the Urnfield period (900-700 B.C.), the Hallstatt period (700-400 B.C.) and the three La Tène periods (400-100 B.C.). The excavations of Manching in Bavaria show in a most impressive manner the Celtic Oppida civilisation of the second and first century B.C. which perished either in Roman or Germanic conquests. The experts believe that at Manching 10,000 Celts, occupying an area of almost 380 hectares, had established a highly organised urban civilisation.

Almost all mono-syllabic river names in Germany are of Celtic origin: the Ruhr, the Rhine, the Lahn and the Main are examples, as are the names Neckar and Isar. Some even see in the term "deutsch" a connection with the Celtic word 'tuath' meaning 'people' or 'volk'.

It needs to be stressed, however, that those Celts who eventually settled on the island baptised *Ierni* or *Iverni* by Ptolemy and (derivatively) *Hibernia* by the Romans most probably did not come from regions that are now German speaking - although we do not know for sure when, from where or which Celtic tribes reached the shores of Ireland.

Nevertheless, many Germans may safely assume that Celtic blood flows in their veins also.

The first documented contacts took place in the period of early Christianisation. After the conversion of the people on the Irish isle by St. Patrick (after 432 A.D.), a strong missionary movement to other countries originated in Ireland.

Its first target was Britain, where in 563 A.D., St. Columba (Irish: *Columcille*) founded a monastery on the isle of Iona, in the Scottish Hebrides.

However, this location was in no way to blame for the Latin misnomer 'scoti' for the Irish. Since the Romans assumed the tribes of Scotland to be the same as their Hibernian neighbours, they grew accustomed to calling the Irish people 'scoti'. This usage lasted as long as Latin was the lingua franca, until its demise at the end of the Middle Ages.

It was about the year 600 A.D. that the first Irish monks arrived on the Continent. They came for two reasons: 'peregrinatio pro amore dei' ('pilgrimage for the love of God') and the biblical mandate (Matthew 28,19) 'docete omnes gentes' ('bring the gospel to all nations').

As a disciple of Columba from Iona, Columbanus (543-615 A.D.), together with twelve Irish followers, left Bangor for France where he founded the monastery of Luxeuil, among others. Expelled from France in 610 A.D., Columbanus went on to the Langobards in Bobbio, Italy, passing through Switzerland and Austria, where two of his fellow monks stayed on; one, St. Gallus (Irish: *Callech*), founded St. Gallen and the other, Bregenz.

A second wave of Irish missionaries followed and, through Western Europe, reached the Eastern regions of the Frankish Empire. In Bavaria the names of Declanus, Marinus and Annianus from the first half of the seventh century are still remembered.

At the time, another Irishman was Abbot at Chiemsee in Bavaria. St. Erhard, St. Emeran and St. Korbian of Freising are also believed to have come from the Emerald Isle. Virgil (Irish: *Fergil*), on the request of the Bavarian Duke Odilo, became the first Bishop of Salzburg. St. Albert, a follower of St. Erhart, whose Vita (1150 A.D.) mentions him as a former

Bishop of Cashel, died in Regensburg, not far from another fellow countryman, St. Alto of Altomunster, in Rheinau near Schaffhausen we find St. Findan.

In Würzburg, however, we find the best-known Irish saints: Kilian, Colman and Totnan. These are said to have been killed there in 689 A.D.. Kilian's importance is attested in the fact that he was one of only two saints from east of the Rhine to merit inclusion in the liturgical calendar of the Frankish kings (the other being Boniface).

In the martyrology of the monk Beda Venerabilis (pre-850 A.D.) the entry for the Eighth of July reads:

"On this day Bishop Kilian was tortured alongside his companions in Kastrum Wirziburg (Würzburg) under the order of Duke Gozbert."

Though there exists no eye witness account of these three martyrs - we must rely on two 9th century manuscripts, the 'passio Kiliani minor' and the 'passio maior' - the impressive long tradition of belief in Kilian leaves us in little doubt as to his historical existence (which some historians question). As early as 752 A.D. the first Bishop of Würzburg, Burghard, had bones attributed to the saints elevated to the honour of the altar. In the presence of Charlemagne these relics were transferred to the newly built Salvator Cathedral in 788.

The reputed motive for the murder of the saints is remarkable and resembles the fate of John the Baptist. St. Kilian is said to have come into conflict with the local ruler, Duke Gozbert of Wircibur (Würzburg), due to a difference of opinion on marriage law. Canon law (based on Lev. 18,16), which St. Kilian defended fervently, forbade marriage between in-laws, whereas Frankish law did not. After the death of his brother there was no obstacle to the Prince's marriage to his sister-in-law Geilana, who, it is rumoured, may have been involved in the sudden death of her husband. Geilana found St. Kilian's attitude rather trying and is thus reputed to have arranged his death.

Eleven Irish Brothers were with the Anglo-Saxon Willibrord while undertaking missionary work in Frisia. Fridolin was with the Alemans, while Dissibold, whose life story was written by Hildegard of Bingen (1170 A.D.), worked as a missionary together with Clement, Griswold and Salust around Trier and Mainz (Dissiboldsberg). In 975 A.D. Martinus founded the famous monastery in Cologne which was named after him and where in 1004 A.D. we come across another Irishman, St. Ailél, as Abbot. The St. Pantaleon Monastery of Cologne was likewise in Irish hands (1042 A.D.). There are said to be over one hundred Irish saints in German speaking countries.

It is no surprise to find so called "Schottenkirchen" or "Schottenklöster" (Scottish churches and monasteries) in many German and Austrian cities even today, all of them actually founded by Irish monks. The Irish who came to continental Europe at that time were renowned not only for their piety but also for their scholarship. Manuscripts written by Irish monks ('libri scotice scripti'), somewhat similar to the Book of Kells, are to be found, amongst other places, in Bamberg, St. Gallen and Schaffhausen. The manuscripts (Letters of St. Paul) at Würzburg with their Gaelic annotations are the most remarkable of all.

There followed a stream of Irish pilgrims on their way to Rome ('Scoti vagantes'). In the tenth and eleventh centuries 'peregrinatio' became almost fashionable. Even kings and princes from Ireland took the route through Germany and Austria. Colman, the son of the High King Malachias, died in Vienna in 1092 A.D. while on such a pilgrimage. He is buried at Melk Monastery in the valley of the Danube. 'Peregrinatio' was often a kind of flight in response to the numerous incursions of the Norsemen or Vikings into Ireland from 795 A.D. onwards. Others from Ireland were attracted less by the Church than by the flourishing Carolingian palace-schools and courts.

The Irish scholar Clemens Scotus had a high reputation at the court of King Lothar. He wrote a scholarly work entitled 'Ars Grammatica' around 830 A.D. In the tenth and eleventh centuries more Irish scholars than priests made their mark in German lands. Discuil, Sedulius Scotus and Johannes Scotus Eriugena merit particular mention. The latter developed a kind of Christian pantheism, which equated God with nature. Marianus Scotus (1082-1128 A.D.) was to become one of the most important historians of the Middle Ages. He wrote a world chronicle that exerted considerable contemporary influence. First a monk at St. Martin's in Cologne, he went on to Paderborn, Fulda and Würzburg before finally settling in Mainz Cathedral as a so-called 'inclusus'.

A second noted scholar went by the name of Marianus Scotus. He arrived from Ireland with two colleagues, Johannes and Candidus, at Michaelsberg in Bamberg in 1067 A.D. Later he moved on to Regensburg, another stronghold of Irish priests and scholars, where after some time as an 'inclusus' he was made Abbot of St. Jakob. The year of his death is disputed, and thought to be either 1083 A.D. or 1086 A.D.

In the same period we know of only one German 'operation' on Irish soil. Between 1127 and 1134 A.D., Cormac MacCarthy of Desmond, King of Munster, had a Romanesque church (*Cormac's Chapel*) built on the Rock of Cashel, then seat of the Irish High Kings. At least two craftsmen from Regensburg in Germany, a carpenter called Conrad and a joiner called William, were recruited. At the behest of the Irish abbot Dirmicius of Regensburg, they arrived together with several monks who were to do some fund-raising with the King. The chapel on the Rock does indeed bear some resemblance to Romanic churches at Regensburg.

2. Medieval Episodes

From the High Middle Ages to the beginning of modern times, there was something of a lull in Irish-German connections. This was probably a result of the Anglo-Norman invasion of the Emerald Isle in 1169 A.D. The struggle of the Irish against their new overlords made it difficult for them to maintain contact with the Continent. Where such contact did take place it tended to be with neighbouring Catholic France. Here, Irish ambition for independence found a natural ally, where uprisings could be plotted and support could be raised, albeit with little success. After the reformation Irish Catholic priests could be trained with less difficulty in France than in Ireland.

After the fifteenth century the Irish associated German lands mainly with Luther's Reformation, or the numerous continental wars involving large mercenary armies. During the Jacobites' war, in which the Catholic King James II was defeated by the Protestant King William III (of Orange) at the Battle of the Boyne on 12 July 1690, quite a number of mercenaries from Hesse and Hanover fought on the Protestant side of the conflict. Their leader was General Frederick, Duke of Schonberg (or Schomberg), born in Heidelberg in 1615. He died at the Boyne and is buried in St. Patrick's Cathedral in Dublin: there is a large stone and an inscription on the wall to serve as a reminder of his role. His popularity at home in Germany seems to have been every bit as limited as with the Catholic Irish.

The peculiar inscription in St. Patrick's which (Protestant) Dean Swift (1677-1745) composed himself in Latin and translated into English reads:

> "Beneath this stone lies the body of Frederick, Duke of Schomberg, who was killed at the Boyne, A.D. 1690. The Dean and Chapter earnestly and

repeatedly requested the Duke's children to undertake the erection of a monument in memory of their father. Long and often they pressed the request by letter and through friends. It was of no avail. At long last, they (the Dean and the Chapter) set up this stone that at least you may know, stranger, where the ashes of Schomberg lie buried. The renown of his valour had greater power among strangers than had the ties of blood amongst his kith and kin. A.D. 1731."

These Teutonic 'dogs of war' had a truly formidable reputation. On the other side the Irish as mercenaries in Continental armies of all shades in the sixteenth and the seventeenth century were not much better. In 1521 the famous German painter Albrecht Dürer produced portraits of such frightening Irish die-hards. During the Thirty Years War (1618-1648), which utterly devastated Germany, there were several prominent Irishmen in Field Marshal Wallenstein's camp: a Walter Butler, a Macdonald, a De Burgh, a Geraldine, a Devereux and Wallenstein's Chaplain Patrick Taaffe. A reading of Schiller's play 'Wallenstein's Camp' is not necessary to know that the Irish colonels killed the Field Marshal in 1634. In a pamphlet of this year the Rector of the Jesuit College in Neuhaus (Bohemia), Caesar de la Couture, accounts the sequence of events. Wallenstein, Duke of Friedland, about to defect from the imperial to the enemy camp, sought from his Irish and Scottish colonels an oath of allegiance. Their loyalty, however, remained firmly with the Emperor and they determined to dispose of the Friedländer forthwith. As de la Couture tells it:

"Taking Eger Castle as his lodgement, Leslie filled it with fifty loyal Irish soldiers, from which the colonels ordered two captains to approach the castle with twenty select Irishmen bearing arms. Devereux rushed at the Friedländer and thrust his halberd into his breast. This took place on 25 February 1634."

A 1688 chronicle of Heidelberg depicts the terror spread by Irish troops during the destruction of the city by the French under General Melac. Not even in Heidelberg's Holy Ghost Cathedral did women and children feel safe.

After their defeat at the Battle of the Boyne in 1690, as is well known, thousands of Irish Jacobites, the so-called 'Wild Geese', fled the Emerald Isle in order to make their living on the Continent, many as soldiers. The Prussian 'Soldier King' Frederick William I (1688-1740) was particularly keen on bringing Irishmen into his beloved guard of so-called 'tall fellows'.

Only an indirectly religious background can be found to the settlement in Ireland of people from the German province of Palatina after 1709. Some thirteen to fourteen thousand resolved to emigrate to the Carolinas in America via Rotterdam and London. Their motive lay primarily in the inconceivable poverty and the destruction caused by numerous incursions into their land by Louis XIV's 'soldadeska', particularly in the Spanish War of Succession. The Palatine Elector Johann Wilhelm, ensconced at a safe distance in Düsseldorf, did not lift a finger to assist his subjects, as Liselotte of Palatina, wife of Louis XIV's brother, lamented in her famous correspondence of 8 October 1695 from Fontainebleu:

> "The Elector of Palatina would do better, before God and the world, to put his funds in the direction of his wretched Palatine people rather than frittering them away on carnival entertainment."

A report from Holland to the English court lends weight to this view, recording that the Palatines had fled in order "to shake off the burden they lie under by the hardship of their Prince's Government and the contributions they must pay to the Enemy."

ଓ

There were also conflicts with their rulers over religious freedom. Whoever was responsible for further transport to America had run out of financial means: the prospective emigrants became stranded in London. Living in tents during the English winter, they suffered untold hardship. They became quite a headache for Londoners and even Queen Anne, who decided to settle them in Ireland.

After the Battle of the Boyne, as well as under Cromwell in 1653, many Catholic landowners, who were considered rebellious, found themselves expropriated. Two hundred and seventy estates passed into Protestant hands, leaving only one third of the land, mostly barren, to Catholics. These new Protestant landlords urgently needed people who would be willing and able to cultivate the recently distributed land and who would strengthen the Protestant element in the country.

The English Parliament debated the plight of the Palatines, coming up with the following resolution on 23 August 1709:

> "That Her Majesty, by sending over a portion of Protestant Palatines into this Kingdom of Ireland, has very much consolidated the strengthening and securing of the Protestant interest in Ireland... that it will very much contribute to the security of this Kingdom, that the said Protestant Palatines be encouraged and settled therein."

Eight hundred and twenty-one families were sent over from London. It was some time before the Commission set up for this purpose had all the families distributed, mainly to County Limerick. For many years after, the English Crown paid a subsidy to the landowners for their assistance in the re-settlement. The work was extremely hard. Many of the Palatines were not farmers but craftsmen. As a result three hundred and twenty five families gave up and moved either back to Britain or on to America, their original destination.

The remaining five hundred and thirty eight families proved to be pious, God fearing, industrious and peaceable people. Very little tension arose between these Protestant Germans and their Catholic Irish neighbours, particularly since the Palatines kept to themselves and rarely married outside their communities.

When in 1842 the German anthropologist J.K. Kohl visited Ireland he asked the Catholic Irish about the Palatines. He reports that *"they enjoy a reputation as the best of farmers and the most honest of people. They are most commendable people."*

ભ

Paul Heyse, the first German ever to receive the Nobel Prize for Literature in 1910, as a young man wrote a play on the Irish Palatines. He was inspired by Victor Aimé Hubert's novel 'The Irish Palatine's Daughter' (in *Tales from Ireland*, 1850). To this day this same theme is the title of a well known Irish folk song.

Most Irish Palatines have since anglicised their names. To give some examples: Schweitzer became *Switzer*, Schultheiß became *Sholdice* or *Shouldice*, Meyer changed to *Myer*. The Bubenhausers adopted the name *Bovenizer*, and the Imbergers *Embury*.

Between 1750 and 1789 the founder of the Methodist Movement, the Englishman John Wesley, tried on many occasions to do missionary work in Ireland. Rather frustrated with the Catholics, he received a more favourable reaction from the pious Palatines. It was Irish Palatine Methodists who were to become so important to the Methodist Church in the USA. A certain Philip Embury emigrated from Ballingrane, Co. Limerick, to New York in 1760 and - with the help of Barbara Hecks, née Ruckle [Röckel], from the same village - founded the Methodist Movement in the USA.

Today the descendants of those Palatines look proudly on their roots and keep alive their traditions within the Irish Palatine Association. At Rathkeale, south of Limerick City, there is a monument to their past in the form of the Irish Palatine Museum.

Catholic Ireland in the eighteenth century would rather have kept her distance from Germany, which was considered a Protestant land. The Protestant upper classes for their part displayed a certain respect for German culture, an attitude fostered in no small part by the ties of the British Crown with Germany. As such they welcomed the foundation of a German Lutheran congregation in Dublin by German merchants as early as 1697. Their 'German Lutheran Church of the Most Holy Trinity' was consecrated in 1725 in Poolbeg Street. The Germans had chosen a clergyman called Lichtenstein as their pastor, a man who had accompanied troops from Brandenburg in the Williamite war. Today this Lutheran community at St. Finian's Church in Adelaide Street considers itself not only as German but as the Irish centre of the world wide family of all Lutherans, although the German Evangelical Church (EKD) is financing St. Finian's as well as its pastor.

Händel, whose Messiah was premiered in Dublin in 1742, was still considered a German at that time, as was originally Sir Richard Castle, the most famous architect of his day in Ireland. Castle was a Huguenot by the name of De Ricardi from the German town of Kassel. Many of the great Irish houses and castles were of his design and are still admired: Powerscourt, Russborough, Carton House, Belvedere, Leinster House as well as parts of Trinity College (the Printing House and Dining Hall). His influence on subsequent architects was immeasurable.

The interest which, during the Seven Years War (1756-63), the Irish showed in Frederick the Great is remarkable. The 'establishment' in Ireland raved about Frederick's victories at Rossbach and Leuthen in the winter of 1757. At this time England was Prussia's ally, a circumstance which manifested itself mainly in British subsidies for the Prussian king. Frederick was considered a great hero in British Ireland because he defeated the French and triumphed in the name of Protestantism over papist Austria and France. The misunderstanding could not have been greater (Frederick was a talented communicator). As is well known, Frederick was a notorious free thinker, and a friend of Voltaire. Religion did not concern him.

In Dublin as in London, Frederick's birthday was publicly celebrated for a few years. Irish pubs were named

'King of Prussia', a Prussian Club founded and a street called 'Prussia Street' was named; it still bears this name today. The enthusiasm faded when, after the resignation of Pitt the Elder (1708-88), London changed its allegiances, cancelled the alliance with Prussia and left Frederick with little good to say about the British.

3. Stormy Times

A turning point in Irish-German ties came, as was the case in so many other contexts, with the American War of Independence (1775-1783) and the French Revolution (1789). The general nationalistic and revolutionary atmosphere seemed also to favour independence for the Irish. The abortive uprising of the republican 'United Irishmen' association in 1793 under the leadership of the Protestant Wolfe Tone had its origin in revolutionary France. Wolfe Tone was, however, also a frequent visitor in Hamburg where his sister lived. Hamburg offered shelter to the exile and his wife after the failure of the uprising. It was considered an ideal place from which to get to Ireland via Britain without being discovered. Wolfe Tone's efforts to gather aid for the Irish cause also brought him to other German towns. The Irish dilemma became evident in one particular incident. When he was dining with a high ranking French official on the bank of the Rhine in Bonn, he saw on the other side a group of Irish Free Corps soldiers wearing their distinctive green jackets and red trousers. They were fighting, not on Wolfe Tone's side, but for the Austrians against the French under the command of an officer named O'Donnell. In August 1797 Wolfe Tone was in Wetzlar to discuss another Irish-French campaign with the French Marshall Hoche, the man whose expedition in 1796 to land at Bantry Bay resulted in failure.

In 1796 the Irish rebels Lord Edward Fitzgerald and Arthur O'Connor spent some time in Hamburg where they negotiated with the French for further support. After the subsequent futile attempt to achieve independence in 1798 Napper Tandy and many of his friends took refuge in Hamburg as well. It was, however, quite a shock to the Irish republican movement when, at the request of the British, the

23

authorities of Hamburg arrested Napper Tandy and the other Irish refugees and extradited them to Britain.

The nineteenth century brought Ireland and Germany closer together, again mainly in the cultural field. As early as 1775 Dublin's Trinity College had started teaching German language and literature. At first the students were almost exclusively theologians. It was their tradition to complement their studies with a journey to Germany where they would follow Luther's tracks. It was only after 1866 that the German Chair at Trinity gained a somewhat wider scope under the famous Professor Maximilian Selss.

In Galway, too, Germanic studies were up and running by the middle of the century, started by Bensbach from 1849-69 and continued respectively by Geisler (1869-86) and Steinberger (1886-90).

Irish interest in German literature took off with the appearance in translation of the work of Klopstock, Goethe, Schiller and other German authors or poets, a breakthrough which we can attribute to the 'Young Ireland' movement and in particular to Clarence Mangan (1803-49) who made the translations and published them in the "Dublin University" magazine and in his "Anthologia Germanica" series (22 instalments between 1835 and 1846). The 'Young Irishmen' around Thomas Davis were particularly enthusiastic. It was their journal 'The Nation', which printed translations of poems by such Germans as Freiligrath, Körner and Rückert. Jane Francesa Elgee, better known as Oscar Wilde's mother, did most of these translations.

Wilhelm von Humboldt's educational reforms in Prussia and of course, Kant's 'Critique of Pure Reason', translated in 1872 by John Pentland Mahaffy, later to become Provost of Trinity, also attracted much attention. It was Mahaffy more than anyone before him who promoted the study of German language and literature.

On the German side this was a period which saw the brothers Grimm edit their *"Irish Fairy Tales"* and von Killinger bring out another collection of traditional Irish stories called *"Erin"*. Both books became quite popular and influenced the image the Germans were to have of the Irish. Goethe's

Werther became standard reading in Ireland. Its influence on such poets as Maria Edgeworth has been repeatedly highlighted.

The romantic movement, which took its origin at least partly from the 'Ossian' poems, (at the time believed to be ancient Celtic but actually written by the Scotsman James Macpherson in 1762-63) seized the imagination of intellectuals in both countries. The strong romantic impact on literature in Germany was reflected in Ireland. The German philosopher Herder's interest in linguistics, his rediscovery of the Middle Ages and therefore also of medieval manuscripts with Gaelic annotations such as at Würzburg, made a considerable impression on the educated classes in Ireland. It was above all his idea of the historical and political importance of 'the nation' as the natural entity of human society that led to a re-orientation of Irish thinking and revived interest in the Irish language. It was only after the French Revolution that a broader German public became aware of the so-called 'Irish Question'. The new era had created the phenomenon of public opinion or rather its enormous importance for politics. Thus at the beginning of the nineteenth century modern journalism was born. All of a sudden the struggle of the Irish Catholics for emancipation and abolition of the old penal laws made the German headlines. When studying the discussion of the time, however, one cannot ignore the fact that misinformation and prejudice were prevalent. Even Goethe cannot be excluded from this statement. In his letters and diaries, 'Maxims and Reflections', as well as his discourse with Eckermann he proves rather biased and anglophile.

Not so his daughter-in-law, Ottilie von Goethe. Her enthusiasm for all things Irish was such that she can easily be considered one of the first 'Ireland fans' in Germany. The reason for this must have been her intimate relationship with the Irishman James Sterling, a theologian, as well as her exchange of ideas with the writer and journalist F.G. Kühne. In 1840 he wrote a three volume novel "Rebels of Ireland" and in 1856 a play called 'The Dublin Conspiracy'. The fact that he was fairly successful attests the growing interest in Irish affairs.

Although he never visited Ireland, the poet, writer and journalist Heinrich Heine also took up the subject of Ireland, though from a political perspective. Critical of England in many respects he followed the fight for emancipation passionately and with much sympathy. In an article he wrote in 1828, long before the Famine, he insisted:

> *"Indeed, the peoples of Europe would have the right to intervene in the cause of Ireland's suffering - with arms, if necessary - and this right would certainly be exerted, were not injustice the stronger force always."*

Due to the anti-religious sentiment of the French Revolution the Irish Church's focus on France came to an end. Therefore it is not remarkable that in the early 1800s contacts between the Irish and the German Catholic clergy became close. As early as 1795 the Maynooth Seminar had begun to play a role in this process. But the hero of the period was, of course, Daniel O'Connell (1775-1847), not only for the Catholic Irish but also for the Catholic Germans. Joseph Görres (1776-1848), the founder of Catholic journalism and the Catholic movement in Germany, was greatly influenced by Daniel O'Connell. It is said that in many Catholic German households a portrait of Daniel O'Connell was standard. Even the Protestant and anglo-phile Goethe mentioned O'Connell, calling him "a brave man".

Besides journalism, which increased Germany's awareness of what was happening in other countries, there was another factor at the end of the eighteenth and the start of the nineteenth century that played an important role. Even before the French Revolution it had become fashionable for wealthy and educated people to go on study tours to foreign lands and to write books about them. Ireland was one of the more popular destinations and subjects of German travel literature. In 1791 the first real Irish travel guide was written by F.G. Krebel. It was preceded by descriptions and reports by J.J. Volkmann (1784) and the much read K.G. Küttner (1785). Later, after the popularity of Krebel's guidebook, came others: P.A. Nemmich (1807), F. von Raumer (1836),

J.G. Kohl (1843), J. Venedey (1844), C. Clement (1845) as well as M. Hartmann (1850). The widest attention, however, was received by Count Pückler-Muskau's *Irish Diaries* of 1826 and 1829. In terms of their influence on Ireland's image in Germany they might be considered a genuine precursor of Heinrich Böll's *'Irish Diary'* of 1957. Pückler's account of his travels was highly subjective and eclectic. He mixed mainly with wealthy Protestant notables and pastors, not least as he was searching for a bride with a handsome dowry. He was not, however, blind to the alarming poverty of the ordinary populace, of which he writes: *"There is no people more poetic and endowed with such rich imagination."* The Protestant Pückler did not simply romanticise Ireland along traditional lines. He observes:

"[that] not even Catholic emancipation could do much. For the real problem is twofold: the lion's share of the land and wealth belongs to the aristocracy, whose interests always send them back to England; and more importantly, the poor Catholic Irish are forced to pay large sums of money each year to the Protestant clergy. As long as this remains the case, things shall hardly flourish."

Karls Marx' partner Friedrich Engels (1820-95) had a most unique connection with Ireland, thanks not least to his two life long partners, the Irish sisters Mary and Lizzy Burns. They came from the family of an Irish textile dyer in Manchester, where the exiled Engels was managing the English branch of his father's business. The relationship with Mary Burns lasted until her death twenty years later, that with Lizzy Burns a further fifteen years. Such closeness to the Burns family played a critical role in bringing the attention of this 'capitalist entrepreneur' to the plight of the proletariat. His 'Irish family' acquainted him with the proletariat's living and working conditions in England, with Engels writing of what he saw to his friend Karl Marx, himself exiled in London without much practical experience of the proletariat.

The influence of the two Irish women also helped generate Engels' lifelong passionate commitment to the cause of the Irish people. Marx' son-in-law, the French doctor Paul Lafargue, recalled that Lizzy (whom Engels formally wedded just hours before her death in 1878) was in "continuous contact with Irish Fenians" and was at all times up to date on their 'plots'. Indeed, more than one Fenian found shelter under Engels' roof.

In May 1856, accompanied by Mary Burns, Engels made his first trip through Ireland. He gave detailed reports of the horrific post-famine conditions there to Karl Marx. He paid a second visit in September 1869 with Lizzy Burns and Marx' daughter Eleonor ("Tussy"). He found things very much the same. These journeys made such a strong impression on Engels that, in the summer of 1870, he set about writing a wide ranging book on Irish history. This project did not pass its initial stages. Engels' third and final journey to Ireland was in September 1891, this time with Louise Kautsky and the Burns' niece Mary Ellen (part of whose childhood was spent living with the Engels). Louise was the divorcée of Karl Kautsky, the German socialist leader (on the revisionist wing) who was, like Marx, living in exile in London. Up to Engels' death in 1895, Louise acted as his housekeeper and private secretary. It was left to Mary Ellen Burns, Louise Kautsky and the Marx children to carry out Engels' last wish in August 1895 - that the urn with his ashes be committed to the depth of the Irish Sea.

03

It is well known in German history that in 1848 the King of Bavaria, Ludwig I, responsible for most of Munich's classicist architecture, fell victim to his affair with a dancer called Lola Montez. Few are aware of the fact that this femme fatale was by no means Spanish as the name suggests but an Irish lass. The name of Lola Montez was meant to be an alias rather than a *nom de plume*. All through her life the lady in question did her utmost to keep her personal background in the dark. In actual fact Lola Montez was born in Limerick in

1820 or 1821 and baptised Eliza Gilbert. Her parents' marriage is well documented in the *Ennis Chronicle* of 6 May 1820. Her father, Edward Gilbert, being an officer in the British Army might have well felt more British than Irish. Her mother, however, was undoubtedly Irish. She was born Elisabeth Oliver, daughter of the wealthy Charles Silver Oliver, MP, of Castle Oliver, an estate at Kil-finane south of Limerick. The young couple's marriage seems not to have been to the liking of the Oliver family. Captain Gilbert volunteered very soon for service in India - in Calcutta and Dinapore - where as early as 1823 he died of cholera. It did not take long for Elisabeth to marry a Scottish officer, Major Patrick Craigie, who was later to become a general. Eliza or Betty, being of school age, was sent first to her stepfather's family in Scotland, and then on to boarding school in England. When Eliza was sixteen her mother, on home leave from India, decided to marry her daughter off as quickly as possible.

The strong willed Eliza, however, refused the chosen bridegroom, a sixty year old judge at Calcutta's Supreme Court. Instead she eloped to Ireland with her mother's protegé, a Captain Thomas James of Wexford, a man in his thirties, also on leave from service in India. The two were married in County Meath by James' brother, a clergyman, in spite of Eliza being a minor. The marriage soon turned out to be a disaster, particularly in India.

In 1840 at the age of twenty, already scandal ridden and with a broken marriage behind her, Eliza James sailed back to Britain. There she was saved from the then consequences of adulterous relationships, namely prison, not by a divorce but a legal separation on her husband's request. The various scandals in India and Britain surrounding the young capricious beauty were, however, widely publicised. Eliza had few options in Victorian England. One possibility was the theatre. She followed the example of Fanny Elßler, lover of Viennese statesman Friedrich von Gentz and chose the career of a dancer. Although little talented, she was of passionate expression and prepared to show more than usual on the stage. She got the idea of adopting a Spanish identity when touring Spain on her only journey there with one of her lovers.

Back in London she encountered bad luck right from the start. The first performance of Lola Montez ended in a scandal - a rejected lover made her real name and adulterous background public. The only choice was to leave England for the Continent. Here the temperamental Irish dancer, whose extraordinary personality was attested by all who knew her, tried her luck in several capitals. Her love affairs with the high and mighty, as well as famous artists including Franz Liszt became the talk of the town. She did her utmost to attract attention by eccentric and scandalous behaviour. Her stays in Brussels, Berlin, Warsaw and Dresden were therefore of short duration. Only in Paris the then twenty three year old Lola seemed to have flourished for a while. There she competed with George Sand in a controversial emancipated lifestyle, associated with the newly rich, the aristocracy and artists such as Paul Méry and Alexandre Dumas. She was close to a lasting relationship with the editor of a major daily newspaper when he perished in a duel for her sake. Again involved in a legal scandal, Lola was forced to leave Paris.

In October 1846, after unsuccessful stays in Bonn and Baden-Baden, Lola Montez turned to Munich. The monarch there was the rather autocratic Ludwig I, known for his love of classicist architecture and building activities as well as for female beauty, namely his gallery of thirty six beauties at Nymphenburg Castle. Lola, her request for performing at Munich's theatres refused, appealed directly to the sixty year old King. On 6 October 1846, she was granted an audience which was to be the beginning of a great romance. Ludwig succumbed totally to the charm of the supposedly Spanish noblewoman (she now called herself Maria Dolores von Porris und Montes) and fulfilled all her wishes, from a generous allowance, a city palace to the title of Countess von Landsfeld, very much against his Court's and the Bavarian Government's advice and gusto.

This might have been accepted as just another costly royal whim had Lola Montez not shown an eager ambition of meddling openly in the political and personnel affairs of her royal lover and his government. She was motivated amongst other things by a profound hatred of all things Jesuit. Her ambition, coupled with her provocative eccentricities, made her an army of enemies. In 1848 a student revolt arising from the dismissal of a number of professors resulted in the closure of the university on Lola's request. This led to a major popular uprising against Lola and the King forcing her to flee Munich. King Ludwig I had to abdicate and leave Bavaria, particularly since the Lola revolt spilled over into the general revolutionary movement of 1848.

Lola, having been denounced for her infidelity to the King during her heyday in Munich, lost Ludwig's favour and support. Lola Montez finally emigrated to Australia and the USA where she survived first as a dancer, not without creating more scandals, then by lecturing on the activities of the European Royal Courts. She died in 1861 in New York, at the age of forty one, in the arms of an Irish clergyman. Ludwig survived her, but died, aged seventy-one, in Nice in 1868.

ରେ

Celtic studies, which were to prove so central in consolidating Irish-German cultural relations and in forming Germany's image in Ireland, started with the Romantic movement and the ideas of Herder. Franz Bopp's call for a scientific study of Celtic languages, made in a Berlin lecture in 1838, set the ball rolling. The publication in 1853 by Caspar Zeuss, a Bavarian schoolteacher, of the 'Grammatica Celtica', written in Latin, caused a huge stir. Zeuss was fascinated by the Gaelic writing on the Würzburg manuscript. In 1864 Kiepert established the connection between the Celtic and the Indo-Germanic languages. In Ireland the blossoming of interest in all this was due above all to the efforts of John O'Donovan who, at Jakob Grimm's suggestion, was made a Corresponding Member of the Royal Prussian Academy in Berlin. Trinity College at this time had two German linguists concentrating on Sanskrit and Celtic, Rudolf Thomas Siegfried and C. F. Lottner. The English linguist Whitley Stokes, a student of Siegfried, brought them into contact with the famous Celtic scholar in Berlin, Ernst Windisch. A whole network came into being.

The remote Aran Islands held a particular attraction for these scholars. The dialect spoken there seemed to be the key to the Celtic language. German professors like Franz Nikolaus Fink, Hermann Osthoff, Heinrich Zimmer and Kuno Meyer were frequent guests of the Aran Islanders. On 27 August 1889, for instance, Kuno Meyer sent Whitley Stokes holiday greetings from the islands:

> "Dear Dr Stokes, we are very happy here...The priest, Father O'Donohue, is most kind to us...Mr Quinn from Liverpool is here also, struggling bravely with the language. I am taking down as many words, phrases etc. as I can pick up. They certainly use fewer English loan words here than in Achill."

In 1892 at Marburg, Fink finally published his comprehensive work on the 'Aran Dialect'. Windisch wrote a 'History of Celtic Philology' in 1880, Alfred Holder his 'Old Celtic Vocabulary' in 1891. In the meantime the 'Journal for Celtic Philology' and the 'Archive for Celtic Lexicography' had been founded in Berlin. All this created a closely knit community of German and Irish linguists. The renaissance of the Irish language and the enormous contribution to it by German scholars such as Windisch and Zimmer, and later Thurneysen and Pokorny, did not reach the consciousness of the broader Irish public until the beginning of the twentieth century and the involvement of Kuno Meyer. The impact he made on Irish-German relations cannot be overestimated. The Irish-German 'Celtic connection', incidentally, did not suffer even in the most difficult of times. When in 1922 the highly respected Thurneysen wanted to publish his 'Celtic Grammar' he could do so only with the financial help of the newly independent Irish Free State. The Germans were broke.

CR

In the second half of the nineteenth century commercial relations intensified. The German Confederation (Deutscher Bund, 1815-1866) and the Second Reich (1871-1918) had

Honorary Consuls in almost all major Irish ports such as Dublin, Belfast, Cork, Limerick, Derry, Waterford and Dundalk.

The late but all the more rapid industrial upsurge in the Germany of the late nineteenth century attracted enterprising Irishmen. The most famous and successful one was without any doubt Dubliner William Thomas Mulvany (1806-1885), the son of a well known painter. A civil engineer at the Board of Works, he had played an important part in the construction of the Irish canal system. At the age of forty-three he went into early retirement, leaving Ireland in 1849 in order to found highly productive underground coal mines in the Ruhr district. He named them Shamrock (1856 at Gelsenkirchen) and Hibernia (1857 at Herne). Later came the mining company Erin, which was taken over by the Prussian State in 1882. Not until the 1970's did the Hibernia pass into the hands of the Ruhr coal concern Veba. An ironworks in Duisburg, the Rhine-Weser-Elbe-Canal, the Midland Canal and the Dortmund-Ems Canal were further results of Mulvany's initiative. He is further remembered as the founder of the Düsseldorf Stock Exchange, where a statue commemorates him, as is also the case at Veba headquarters. Mulvany died in 1886 in Düsseldorf an extremely rich and highly respected man, and was buried in that city.

The Germans, most of all the Catholics, followed the Irish Question after the Famine with great sympathy and understanding. On the purely political front, however, the Irish problem remained an element of German relations with Great Britain. On the other hand the image of Germany and the Germans held by the Irish was still determined by religious considerations. The Franco-German War of 1870-71 therefore was seen by the Catholic Irish less as a struggle for German unity than as a conflict between the Catholic Celtic brotherly nation France and Protestant Prussia.

The Irish demonstrated their feelings by sending a corps of medics to the French front. When the German Honorary Consul in Limerick, an Irish Palatine called Spraight [derived from *Specht*], hoisted the Prussian flag (which he was entitled to do) the population hissed. The only pro-

Prussian demonstrations in 1871 were in Protestant Enniskillen and Ballymena in what is now Northern Ireland.

What interested the Irish after the foundation of the Second Reich was the so-called "Kulturkampf" i.e. Chancellor Bismarck's conflict with Catholicism. When the German Catholics 'won' and Bismarck came to an accommodation with the Church in 1878 under the reign of Pope Leo XIII, this had a considerable and positive impact on Irish Catholics. The image of Germany as an arch-Protestant country changed and improved dramatically, all the more so as the Irish Church was becoming rather disenchanted with growing liberalism in France and with France's policy of secularisation.

In this phase, the fin de siècle, in which the zeitgeist became more and more nationalistic, the Irish were seriously pre-occupied with 'finding themselves' and achieving a distance from Britain.

The economic and political success of the Second Reich made Germany increasingly interesting to Irish nationalists, both those who were for Home Rule and those who demanded a radical separation from Britain. Many saw in Germany's historical development a model for Ireland's own potential. In a relatively short space of time Germany had succeeded in transforming herself from a predominantly agricultural country into an industrial superpower. Now the Germans even challenged what was seen as Britain's search for hegemony in Europe.

Given this, it was no wonder that, for instance, Arthur Griffith of the Irish independence movement Cumann na nGaedheal and later Sinn Féin intensively studied the German model, most of all the economic theories of the German economist Friedrich List. An Irish-German concord came about in October 1899 when the Irish republican movement decided to send an Irish Brigade under John MacBride to join the Germans in supporting the Boers against the British.

At the end of the 19th and at the beginning of the 20th century the room for manoeuvre remained, however, extremely limited. The emphasis on Irish-German ties was as before restricted to the field of culture. In 1884 Michael Cusack, under the influence of Turnvater Jahn's movement in Germany, founded the Gaelic Athletic Association (GAA). In 1883 Douglas Hyde (married to Luzy Curtz, the daughter of a German family from Württemberg which emigrated to London in 1815), later President of Ireland from 1938 to 1945, set up Conradh na Gaeilge, the Gaelic League which, right from the beginning was in contact with the German Celtic scholars.

In this period the influential National Literary Society around W.B. Yeats and T.W. Rolleston showed a keen interest in German Literature. In the USA the idea of close cooperation between Irish-Americans and German-Americans gained ground. But the most prominent figure of all in this cultural exchange was Kuno Meyer. When in 1898 the School Commission in Dublin planned to remove Irish once again from the school curriculum Douglas Hyde sent an appeal for support against the plan to all the Celtic scholars of Europe. He was especially impressed by the ready support of Kuno Meyer (then lecturer of German at Liverpool University). In 1901 Meyer and Zimmer took part in the first Pan-Celtic Congress in Dublin. Again Kuno Meyer left a most positive impression. In his speech to Congress participants Kuno Meyer said, amongst other things:

> *"I have never yet known the Irishman or Irishwoman who were not in their hearts proud of their beautiful native land, and loved it with a far-brought love, a love out of the storied past [...] From this love will spring a wider and greater Ireland than an island of party and faction. I do not despair that even Professor Mahaffy [Provost of Trinity College] whose brilliant wit and ready satire too often give the lie to his true Irish heart, will be a content citizen of that greater Ireland."*

In 1903 Douglas Hyde finally asked Kuno Meyer to become the first director of the newly founded School of Irish Learning in Dublin. Meyer transformed this initially very modest Institute into a leading research centre. He also worked tirelessly for the Gaelic League. In April 1912 the City of Dublin and in September 1912 the City of Cork made him Honorary Citizen. No single German had hitherto done more for the image of Germany cherished by the Irish public. During World War I both cities were forced to withdraw this honour from the 'enemy' Kuno Meyer. But after independence both Dublin and Cork re-instated him promptly. It was to be a posthumous honour.

Kuno Meyer, considering Celtic studies to involve a cultural and even a 'völkische' mission, was in close contact with pan-German circles when he took over Zimmer's Celtic Chair at the University of Berlin in 1911. In those years he was a good friend of Sir Roger Casement, as were his sister Toni and his brother Eduard. Casement helped Meyer establish valuable contacts in the USA where he went in November 1914 after the outbreak of World War I. His mission there was not only to lecture at various universities but to see to it that Irish-American circles stayed on a 'pro-German' course and an anti-German alliance between Britain and the US did not come about. When the US entered the war in 1917 Meyer returned to Germany where he continued to speak in his lectures for the Irish nationalist cause.

Relations between Ireland and Germany before World War I were shaped not only by Kuno Meyer but also by other personalities. The German community in Ireland which hitherto consisted mainly of craftsmen (watchmakers, jewellers, tailors, butchers, cooks etc.) and governesses was reinforced by artists, mainly musicians. The first to arrive, in 1888, was Heinrich Bewerunge (born 1862) from Westfalia, on a post teaching music at Maynooth College. In Cork a virtual tradition of German church music was inaugurated by organist Theo Gmür and Conrad Swartz who were followed by Aloys Fleischmann. Fleischmann was not only a great and popular musician, he also founded a School of Music that served as a model for the teaching of music in the whole of Ireland. He died in 1973, leaving a son to carry on the tradition.

Between 1887 and 1891 a German Dominican Father Thomas Esser became a famous teacher of philosophy at Maynooth. Through him the links between the Irish and the German Catholic Church became closer. Pilgrimages to Maria Laach, Würzburg, Regensburg and Oberammergau became almost fashionable.

4. The Great War and the Casement Story

It was after 1912 that Irish-German relations became political in the proper sense of the word. The key figure in this was Sir Roger Casement (1864-1916), an Anglo-Irish Protestant from County Antrim. Casement, having been a Consular Officer in the British Civil Service, returned to Ireland in order to devote himself exclusively to the republican-nationalist Irish independence movement. With German-British relations becoming increasingly tense, Casement could no doubt be considered pro-German.

At first involved in Irish-German commercial relations, Casement, like the nationalist leader Arthur Griffith, studied the theories of the German economist Friedrich List. A project of Casement's to divert the Hamburg-America shipping traffic from Southampton to the Irish port of Cobh almost succeeded but had to be stopped because of the start of World War I.

In November 1913 the Irish-British conflict reached such a pitch that both Irish parties formed paramilitary organisations, the republicans forming the Irish Volunteers, the loyalists the Ulster Volunteers. Their main difficulty was arms procurement. Both turned to Germany. The unionist leaders Edward Carson and James Craig were determined to stymie the plan for Irish Home Rule by all available means. Their slogan was "Home Rule is Rome Rule". As early as 1911 Carson went so far as to declare in the British Parliament that he would prefer Kaiser William II to the Irish republican leader John Redmond, should the latter become Prime Minister of Ireland. In Carson and Craig's circles the idea was mooted of asking the Protestant powers of continental Europe like Germany for help should there be a majority for Home Rule at Westminster. Indeed in 1913, Carson, a frequent visitor to such spas as Baden-Baden and

Bad Homburg, met with Kaiser William II there. He is said to have told the Kaiser that he could count on many friends in Northern Ireland should there be a war. In fact, both parties subsequently purchased arms in Germany, albeit covertly. In early 1914 the Unionist Ulster Volunteers bought 35,000 German Mauser guns and rifles plus 2½ million rounds of ammunition, which landed at Larne, north of Belfast. In July of the same year it was the nationalists' turn, if on a more modest scale. Nine hundred German guns and 25,000 rounds of ammunition reached Howth near Dublin in the yacht named *Asgard,* owned by the main organiser, Robert Erskine Childers. It was characteristic of the situation even at that time that the British security forces tried hard to confiscate the arms landed at Howth whilst turning a blind eye to those destined for the Unionists.

Immediately after the outbreak of World War I the leader of the Irish nationalists, John Redmond, assured the British of his Party's full support for their war efforts. His suggestion that in order to reduce Britain's burden the defence of Ireland should be left to an Irish force combined from the Ulster and the Irish Volunteers was turned down. His war support declaration and proposal led to a split in the nationalist camp. The majority of the nationalists, including most Irish Volunteers, stood behind Redmond.

A militant minority, however, was determined not to support Britain, preferring instead to seek contact with the German Reich and to use the war for an armed uprising of the Irish people. Their motto was 'Britain's peril is Ireland's opportunity'. Besides Roger Casement, most of the more prominent figures belonged to this second camp: Patrick Pearse, Joseph Plunkett, Thomas MacDonagh, Eoin MacNeill and others either from the Irish Republican Brotherhood (IRB) or from Sinn Féin (SF).

Of the approximately 178,000 National (formerly Irish) Volunteers only about 10,000 joined the British Army - conscription did not apply in Ireland. Due to the difficult economic living conditions in Ireland it was, at least until April 1916, not too difficult to find other Irish volunteers. According to some estimates 90,000 to 100,000 Irishmen fought for the British between 1914 and 1916.

All in all the general mood of the Irish during World War I, though not pro-British, was by no means pro-German. It is said that shopkeepers suspected of German connections were even harassed. The radical wing of the republican minority however, which Casement represented, put its money on Germany. Redmond's policy had also seriously disappointed the Irish-Americans who, under the leadership of John Devoy and McGarrity, were a reliable source of financial support. Immediately after the outbreak of the war, Casement went to the USA with the aim of securing finances. There, together with Devoy and McGarrity, Casement maintained close contact with the German Embassy in Washington, where Count Bernstorff was Ambassador and von Papen, subsequently Chancellor in 1932 and instrumental in Hitler's rise to power, was the Military Attaché.

Money was not all they were concerned with. In Washington, Casement and Devoy drafted amongst other letters to the Reich's Government, a petition to the Kaiser asking him to include Ireland's liberation into the war aims of the Central Powers. In this context Casement proceeded in October 1914 to Germany, where he arrived on 1st November. By the twelfth he had succeeded in concluding an agreement with the Under-Secretary of the German Foreign Office, Arthur Zimmermann. In this document the Germans promised to support morally any future Irish government in her efforts to establish an independent Irish State. On 28th December 1914, this declaration of intent was amended by the decision to form an Irish Brigade for an Irish war of independence, composed of Catholic Irish who had served in the British Army and been made prisoners of war. Upon Casement's suggestion the agreement was extended to the effect that deployment of such forces was also possible in other struggles for independence from Britain. They had Egypt particularly in mind. Casement had obviously not discussed this clause with his friends at home, he had gone it alone.

The Irish Brigade was a failure of the first order. Not more than fifty-five prisoners volunteered, in spite of the fact that Casement himself visited the camps and that two Dominican priests, Fathers Crotty and O'Gorman, had already been called to Germany from Rome to look after the Irish troops. Casement did at least achieve special treatment for all Irish in the PoW camps whether they joined the Brigade or not. The Brigade was eventually stationed in the Danzig area and dissolved itself in the course of the war.

There is an interesting footnote to this episode: the uniform of the Irish Army after 1922 was modelled on the uniform of Casement's Irish Brigade.

Casement was rather frustrated and switched his attention to the arms question. In April 1915 he was joined in Berlin by Joseph Plunkett for a discussion of the armed uprising planned for Dublin. The German arms delivery was to be co-ordinated with the revolt. Much to their disappointment the Germans refused to put military personnel i.e. officers, at their disposal. Arms were all that were agreed to. Casement assumed that he would get 200,000 rifles and machine guns. In actual fact, without Casement's knowledge Devoy had settled for less. Only 20,000 guns plus ammunition left Wilhelmshaven on the German *MS Libau*, disguised as the Norwegian freighter 'Aud'. Casement felt betrayed.

The *Aud/Libau* reached Tralee Bay on Holy Thursday 1916. Since she was not equipped with wireless she remained uninformed of the decision taken by Devoy to delay the unloading to Easter Sunday. After a day of dangerous waiting the *Aud/Libau* was seized by the British Navy who led her into Cobh harbour. There the ship's captain, Karl Spindler, managed to sink the ship, arms freight and all.

Casement, who had no idea of what was happening, was meanwhile making his way in the German submarine U19 together with Robert Monteith, an exiled instructor of the Irish Volunteers, and a man of the German Irish Brigade named Bailey. They were put on land at Banna Strand near Tralee.

A minor part in this submarine operation was played by a young navy officer by the name of Ernst Heinrich von Weizsäcker, who is remembered for two things: he went on to become State Secretary at Hitler's Foreign Office. He was the father of Richard Karl von Weizsäcker, born in 1920, later to become President of the Federal Republic of Germany.

When Casement landed at Banna Strand it was Good Friday 1916. Due to its wide visibility the location proved unsuitable for such an operation. Casement and his men were discovered and arrested in no time. Casement was taken to London where he was sentenced to death for high treason and hanged on 3rd August, 1916. It was only in 1965 that it became possible to give him a State funeral at Glasnevin Cemetery in Dublin.

The 1916 Easter Rising, which started at Dublin's General Post Office, took place without Casement and the German weapons. As heroic as it was, it ended in disaster. Incidentally, the Irish plans for the insurrection had been discovered by the British a few days previously, following a raid in New York on the office of a German official who was in contact with Devoy. No more than a few of the leaders of the radical republican movement survived, amongst them Eamon De Valera, thanks to his American citizenship. The brutal reaction on the part of the British led to a tremendous increase in sympathy for the radicals in Ireland. Public feeling in the USA rose to great heights of passion. Although any German part in the rebellion during World War I had virtually come to an end, the British continued to suspect that IRB and Sinn Féin were continuing to co-operate closely with Berlin. In actual fact, Sinn Féin had decided at this stage to adopt a neutral stance.

When in April 1918, in the midst of the Irish struggle against British conscription, another member of the former German Irish Brigade, Joseph Dowling, was dropped by a German submarine at Galway Bay and made contact with the local Sinn Féin, the British seized this opportunity, under the pretext of a 'German plot', to arrest not only Dowling but almost all Sinn Féin leaders, amongst them de Valera, Arthur Griffith and Countess Markievicz.

A last attempt at German-Irish contact during the war was made in October 1917 in Geneva. Terence MacSwiney, who was later to become Lord Mayor of Cork and to die of a hunger strike in a British prison, was an in-law of the German Representative in Bern, Rombach. Through him MacSwiney tried to contact the German Government once again and plead assistance for the Irish nationalists, but to no avail. The Casement fiasco had put Berlin on its guard.

The lengths to which the thinking and planning of the Irish nationalists went to achieve maximum benefit for Ireland from the war are shown by yet another episode. At least three of the leaders of the Easter Rising, Thomas Clarke, Joseph Plunkett and Patrick Pearse, thinking of the restoration of the monarchic 1782 constitution with its King, Lords and commons, toyed with the idea of proposing a German prince as Head of State of an independent Ireland. The reasoning was that in the case of a German victory over Britain a close association with Germany might be desirable or necessary. As a candidate the sixth and youngest son of Kaiser William II, Prince Joachim (1890-1920), was mooted. This rather curious case shows how the term 'republican' was understood in these circles. It was a synonym for national emancipation, not the refusal of any monarchic form of State.

A few weeks before the November revolution in Berlin brought the war to an end, a German submarine sank the RMS Leinster mid-way between the Welsh port of Holyhead and the Irish coast, one hour off the Dublin port of Dun Laoghaire (on 11 October 1918). Of 771 passengers (482 of which were soldiers), 501 passengers drowned. This incident represented the last of its kind during the war. Whether this terrible event delayed the ceasefire negotiations already started by Chancellor Prince Max of Baden on 4 October 1918 and therefore was responsible for even more senseless killing, is not clear.

5. Weimar

After World War I the situation in Germany as well as in Ireland underwent a drastic change. A completely new chapter in Irish-German relations had started. Following the revolution in Berlin, the Social Democrat Scheidemann proclaimed Germany a republic. The Kaiser went into exile in Holland. A constitution was drafted in Weimar and accepted. The steeple-chase of the Weimar Republic that was to last almost thirteen years had begun.

In Dublin thirty of the seventy-three Irish MPs in the British House of Commons, thirty-six of whom were in prison, formed an Irish Parliament, Dáil Éireann. The atmosphere was characterised on the one hand by euphoria at Woodrow Wilson's idea of self-determination and on the other by the reality of increased repression by the British. At the first session of the Dáil on 21 January 1919 in Dublin's Mansion House, the independence of the Irish Republic was proclaimed. Eamon de Valera, Arthur Griffith and Count Plunkett (father of Joseph, killed after the Easter Rising) were to represent the Irish State at the Paris Peace Conference. But all three were in British prisons. Thus the Dáil decided to send Séan T. O'Kelly, later President, and George Gavan Duffy. On 3 February 1919, de Valera managed to escape from Lincoln Prison. On 1 April 1919 the Dáil elected him President and Head of Government, whereupon he formed the first cabinet, appointing Count Plunkett as Foreign Minister.

The Irish Republic, as it was then called, was seeking immediate international recognition. At the Versailles Conference, however, delegates were wary of the various German connections of those who were now calling the shots in Dublin, and also mindful of the presence of the victorious British, thus impeding any attempt at diplomatic recognition. Even US President Woodrow Wilson proved to be of little help to the Irish. In June 1919 the Conference decided not to admit the Irish delegates. As the British declared Dáil Éireann a body dangerous to the State, O'Kelly and Gavan Duffy were expelled from France.

They immediately turned to Berlin. However, due to the political turbulence and confusion there, they achieved little. In February 1921 Gavan Duffy again returned to Berlin, now a special envoy of the Dáil. He met with Foreign Minister Gustav Stresemann, who could do no more than explain the difficult situation facing the Weimar Republic. It came as small consolation that during his stay in Berlin Gavan Duffy was given a splendid dinner by the German-Irish Association, where the Celtic scholar Professor Julius Pokorny's speech in perfect Gaelic impressed everybody.

In May 1921 the Dáil sent a memorandum to the Reichstag, the German Parliament, pleading for recognition of the Irish Republic. It was not forthcoming. The German Government, wrestling with the Versailles Treaty powers, was in no position to affront Great Britain. On the contrary, German politicians were hoping to get Britain's support against France in requesting a moderation of the strict Versailles conditions.

In Berlin Ireland had considerable influence. Already during the war, on the initiative of Casement and John Gaffney, a German-Irish Association had been founded on 13 February 1916. On the board sat various dignitaries: two important Members of Parliament, the Centre Party politician Erzberger and the Conservative von Westarp, as well as the famous Baron von Richthofen. The Kaiser had sent his greetings in typical style:

"His Majesty follows the struggle for liberation of brave Ireland with interest and lively sympathy, in full awareness that the German sword has led many a nation to liberty"

The Association, at Berlin's Knesebeckstraße, managed by George Chatterton-Hill and Agatha Grabisch, issued a monthly journal 'Irische Blätter' (Irish Bulletin), which gave information about Irish events along radical republican lines as well as anti-British propaganda. In June 1918, the Association fell into crisis because of differences of opinion between the board members. Erzberger was accused of the politics of "renunciation and of conciliation towards Britain", and was duly expelled. The dormant Association was resurrected after the war. The chair was then filled by Agatha Grabisch, an American lady, who had helped Casement with the Irish Brigade and who was married to a former General Staff advisor. The Association had close contacts with the extreme rightist 'pan-Germanic' circle headed by Dietrich Schäfer and Theodor Schiemann.

With the help of the Association an Irish office was opened in Berlin. It was intended to be an unofficial Embassy. In April 1921 Nancy Wyse-Power, a former postgraduate student of the Celticist Pokorny, was engaged to manage the office. Pokorny and his student Micheál O'Briain assisted.

The Dáil sent out a former British civil servant, John Chartres, in June 1921, who lived at the Hotel Eden until mid-1922. In November 1921, the office gained another Irish recruit, Charles Bewley, later Ambassador to the Vatican and Berlin. He was considered an expert in international trade. From a political point of view all of this came to nothing. In 1923 the frustrated Bewley returned to Dublin, to be replaced by Cornelius Duane. However he, too, gave up at the end of this year at the height of Germany's hyper-inflation.

In contrast to the Irish office, of which only Nancy Wyse-Power remained, the Association lived on. It even managed to organise a memorial service for Casement at Berlin's Hedwigs Cathedral on 3 August and one for Terence MacSwiney on 31 December 1921. Both events were extremely well attended.

The German authorities though were worried about these activities. In an official communication of November 1921, the German Foreign Office requests the Ministry of the Interior to observe the activities of a certain "Fräulein Nanzy Poviard [clearly Nancy Wyse-Power] who runs a German Office for Information from Ireland at the Hardenberg Hotel and issues an *Irish Bulletin*". A response to this request has yet to be discovered.

All the efforts on the part of the Irish failed due to the German Reich's policy of shielding itself from France's 'revanche' and of shaking off or at least reducing the yoke of Versailles by establishing good relations with Britain. Britain for her part was watching any Irish-German contact with the greatest of suspicion. As late as August 1921 Berlin was accused in the House of Commons of supporting Sinn Féin, something the Reich denied vigorously.

In actual fact, the purchase of arms for Ireland was, unofficially, a very topical subject at the time. There was considerable demand for arms in the Irish underground or later during the Irish Civil War. The sale of German arms, however, had been forbidden by the Versailles Treaty. This led to smuggling, which seemed to have been easy enough. The German police were not blind. Even Irish contact with 'Bolshevik circles' was reported by them. The authorities, however, did not feel bound too much by the terms of Versailles.

A major role in the arms trade was played by Robert Briscoe, who before the war had maintained good trade relations with Germany, along with Charles John McGuinness and Séan MacBride. The latter was the son of the famous freedom fighter and femme fatale Maud Gonne and of John MacBride. Séan MacBride was later to distinguish himself as Foreign Minister in the first Irish coalition government, as a human rights campaigner and as a recipient of the Nobel Peace Prize.

In the context of their arms deals, McGuinness was even arrested once and fined two thousand Reichsmark which, thanks to the inflation in Germany, equalled no more than £10. British observers ensured they were present at the trial and were outraged by the ridiculous outcome. Of all the numerous transactions, that of November 1921 is recorded in particular detail: 1,500 German rifles and 1.7 million rounds of ammunition reached the Irish Republic safely.

At the beginning of 1922 the Irish Republic, having lost out to British military force, became the 'Irish Free State', with a dominion-status similar to that of Canada. The acceptance of this minor status of a State and the partition of the island led ultimately to civil war. The provisional Irish Government's ambition under W.T. Cosgrave was modest but realistic. Cosgrave declared:

"Our foreign policy, other than commercial, would be a matter of no importance."

Gavan Duffy, having in the meantime become Cosgrave's Foreign Minister, disagreed and resigned. Desmond Fitzgerald took over. The opponents of the Anglo-Irish Treaty led by Eamon de Valera did not lose any time in building up relations of their own with Germany as well as the USA. Thanks to considerable financial support from the Irish-Americans the flow of German arms for the radicals continued. With the help of such pioneers as Robert Briscoe and John McGuinness there was also a flourishing of normal trade. Briscoe went into partnership with a Berlin trading firm. McGuinness became the owner of the new Irish commercial navy's first ship, which he baptised 'City of Dortmund'. T.D. Liam de Róiste, too, worked with a Berliner, Paul Funke, to set the wheels of German-Irish trade in motion.

Despite the lack of formal diplomatic relations there were, nevertheless, many other unofficial and private contacts made during the twenties. In July 1922 the Chairman of the Irish Constitutional Committee asked for material on the Weimar Constitution. He went through the proper channels, lodging a request with the German Embassy in London. The instruction issued to the Embassy read:

"Any direct contact of official bodies with representatives of the Irish people are, as far as possible, for the time being to be avoided."

Once again, the sensitivities of the British over matters Irish was cited. The requested material did reach its destination however, through other, unofficial channels.

A meeting took place in the summer of 1923 between Irish representatives and Hitler but, given Hitler's low profile at the time, this remained a rather unimportant episode although it might have influenced the Führer's image of Ireland at a later stage.

The promotion of the Irish cause in Germany was carried on tirelessly by writer and poet Francis Stuart, and by rather leftist IRA men like Séan MacBride and Donal O'Donoghue. Both later participated in the Congress of the Anti-Imperialist League in Frankfurt, in July 1929, as another leading member of the IRA, Peadar O'Donnell, did in the European Farmers' Congress in Berlin of May 1930.

In August 1927 the then Adjutant General of the Irish Army, Brennan, made a request, again through the German Embassy in London, to be allowed study the training programme of the Reichswehr. At first he was met with the standard refusal. The reply of the 'Truppenamt' of the Reichswehr Ministry, headed by General von Blomberg (later to be Hitler's first Minister of War), ran:

"Request refused. The competent authority would be the Military Attaché of the British Embassy in Berlin. Furthermore impossible, since none of the powers occupying the Rhineland has ever been admitted to training programmes of the Reichswehr."

After much hesitation the Foreign Office came up with a charming compromise which is indicative of the contemporary style of operating. General Brennan, on the occasion of a private visit to Germany, was to be accompanied by an Attaché, one Count Strachwitz, dined by a captain of the Reichswehr, one von Kaufmann, and shown the Grenadier barracks of Dresden by a Captain Boerstling.

Less complicated was de Valera's first visit to Berlin in 1928 because he was there as a member of the Inter-Parliamentary Union. After all, on the invitation of the Royal Dublin Society, German officers came to Ireland for the first time in 1929 to attend the Dublin Horse Show. Less successful was the Irish attempt to procure German steel helmets for the Irish Army from Germany. In an ironic twist, they had to be manufactured in Britain, based on the German model.

CR

A particularly memorable Irish-German event took place when the first transatlantic crossing by plane from east to west, the counterpart of Lindbergh's famous journey of west to east, took place in 1928. The heroes of this daring enterprise were Commandant Fitzmaurice of the Irish Air Corps and two Germans, Baron von Hünefeld and Captain Köhl. On 12 April, 1928, the three started out from Baldonnel, near Dublin and landed 36 hours later on Newfoundland's Greenly Island. The achievement strengthened not only Irish self-esteem but also Ireland's image in Germany.

On a private and economic level Irish-German contacts continued smoothly. During the Twenties the number of Germans coming to and residing in Ireland increased steadily, due not least to lack of Irish expertise in some fields. At the beginning of 1923 General Richard Mulcahy asked the German Colonel Fritz Brase to come to Dublin and build up Irish military music. Brase requested the assistance of Captain Sauerzweig. Both founded the Irish Army School of Music. In no time Brase's Army Number One Band became extremely popular. Few individuals have done more to foster a positive image in Ireland of Germany than Brase. Upon his retirement in 1940 he handed the School over to Sauerzweig who himself left only seven years later. However, it should be noted that Brase, being the nationalist he was, had been involved in building up the local cell of the Nazi Party (NSDAP) in Dublin after 1933. De Valera having confronted him on the matter, Brase prudently opted for music over Party.

The National Museum of Ireland too, owes its early development to two German directors: Walter Bremer, who died in 1927, followed by the pre-historian and Celtic scholar Dr. Adolf Mahr. The achievements of the eminent musician Aloys Fleischmann, who died in Cork in 1973, are not forgotten, particularly as the good work of music education was carried on by his son, who himself died in 1995.

49

The artistic, if controversial, W. Paffrath manufactured countless plaster madonnas and saints for Catholic churches all over Ireland, which to this day are full of examples of this type of 'art'. Böll's *Diary* carries a remark on Paffrath's work:

> *"Some people - one of them a German, I am told, who has spread the blessings of German culture all over Ireland - must be making a fortune out of plaster figures."*

Paffrath's figures, hollow as they were, are said to have served well for smuggling whiskey from Northern Ireland into the Republic.

⊂⊃

In the economic field, in the framework of de Valera's policy of autarchy, the merits of German specialists should be mentioned as well. A Dr Mecking helped found and organise the Irish Peat Board, Bord na Mona, while a Dr Reinhart laid the foundations for a proper National Forestry Organisation. Dr Winkelmann revived the Irish Glass Bottle Factory. F. Schubert did the same with Solus, the light bulb factory. George Fäsenfeld managed the Roscrea Meat Factory, founded by Séan Lemass. The Allies, buying meat from Roscrea, were afraid of Fäsenfeld poisoning their food, so in 1943 he had to resign. He took up the production of pharmaceuticals as an alternative.

A very special and unique contribution to the strengthening of Irish-German relations was the building of the hydro-electric power station at Ardnacrusha on the Shannon between 1925 and 1929. This power station made electrification on a wider national scale possible and constituted a major modernisation programme for the predominantly agricultural Ireland. The idea to build such a power station originated with the Irish physicist Thomas MacLaughlin, who, first a teacher in Galway, went in the early twenties to Berlin to work for Siemens. His personal acquaintance with the then Minister for Industry and Trade,

Thomas McGilligan, a school friend, may have influenced the positive acceptance of the project by the Irish Government. Tenders were invited and were forthcoming from Norway, Sweden, Switzerland and Germany, but not Britain. Siemens-Schuckert won the contract with an estimated cost of £5.2 million. It was a courageous though not uncontroversial decision given the fact that the annual budget of the Free State was only around £25 million. With the blessing of the Bishop of Killaloe, Dr Fogarty, the contract was concluded on 13 August 1925. Three years and eleven months later the sluice gates were opened, on 22 July 1929.

The project meant that more than three hundred German engineers and technicians were brought to the Shannon region, with hundreds of Irishmen receiving training on the job. The German image was formed anew not only in the Shannon area but all over the country since the project included the building of countless transformer and transmitter stations as well as the laying of 2000 km of cables. Numerous friendships and not a few Irish-German marriages were a pleasing by-product. There were also, however, voices to be heard warning of a loss of distinct Irish identity. The Shannon project did, of course, influence the Irish-German balance of trade. It was in fact a pronounced imbalance. Imports from Germany rose from £744,580 in 1924 to £1,329,931 in 1930, whilst exports to Germany amounted to only £237,981, a figure that had all the same increased fivefold.

The first official treaty between Ireland and Germany was the Trade and Shipping Agreement of 1930. It was the first such treaty ever concluded by the Free State. Trade became more and more important for Ireland. Irish representatives of the Industrial Development Agency (IDA) and many Irish businessmen were regular visitors to the Leipzig Fair. Germany grew to be Ireland's second most important trading partner outside the Commonwealth, ranking only after Britain.

It should also be noted that the Free State had renounced any share in German reparation payments in the early Twenties. Immediately after becoming Head of

Government, de Valera expressed the view that Germany's reparation obligations should be cancelled altogether.

It was only in 1929 that diplomatic relations between Ireland and Germany were formally established. As a Dominion of the British Commonwealth, Ireland had been represented in Berlin by the British Embassy. After this date, the modalities of the Dominion status having been changed, each Dominion was entitled to enter into separate relations. However, there were consular relations which resulted in the opening of a German Consulate General in Dublin as early as 1923. The first Consul General, Dr Georg von Dehn-Schmidt, was already in charge of Irish affairs as Consul in Liverpool prior to moving to Dublin. Consul von Dehn-Schmidt, who was upgraded to Minister Plenipotentiary in 1930, was to represent the Reich's interests until 1934.

Feelings towards Ireland, particularly in Catholic Germany, are reflected in a letter addressed by the Bavarian Prime Minister Hugo Count Lerchenfeld to Foreign Minister Walter Rathenau on 4th April 1922. He wrote:

"The appointment of a prominent Catholic to the post of our General in Dublin appears to me to be of importance. The Catholic element in the cultivation of relations between Germany and Ireland promises to bear good fruit."

In 1930 an Irish Embassy was established in Berlin. The first Minister Plenipotentiary appointed was Professor Daniel A. Binchy, a scholar of high renown, who spoke fluent German and had written his doctoral thesis on the Irish Benedictines of Regensburg. At the age of 24 he had been the youngest Professor of Law at Trinity College Dublin. Characteristic of the legal situation in which Ireland found herself was Binchy's letter of accreditation. It began: *"H.M. the King of Great Britain and Ireland and of the British Dominions Overseas, Emperor of India ..."*

Binchy was held in high regard in Berlin but he did not feel at ease in his new role. By 1932 he had already returned to academic life. One anecdote relates that, when in the

Reich's President Hindenburg's ante-chamber in order to hand over his letter of accreditation, he suddenly realised that he had left the document in his hotel room. A rather speedy operation was required to cover up the folly.

Simultaneously with the setting up of the Irish office in Berlin, von Dehn-Schmidt's Consulate was raised to the status of Embassy. Here too, not everything went smoothly. The bureaucracy in Berlin was pretty slow in finalising the formalities for the upgrading in Dublin. The Irish had to ask repeatedly for speedier action since the French were waiting in the wings and the Irish were determined to have the German Embassy opened before the French.

Soon after formalising relations the Government of the Reich invited the Irish Foreign Minister, also Minister for Industry and Trade, and his spouse together with Permanent Secretary Joseph Walshe. The visit took place between 26 and 29 May 1931. As was customary, counterinvitations were extended to Chancellor Brüning and Foreign Minister Curtius. Due to the turbulence shaking the Weimar Republic in its terminal phase of 1932, their visit was cancelled.

6. De Valera and the Third Reich

In both Germany and Ireland the world economic crisis of 1929 led to major changes in many areas of economic and social activity. In Ireland, there were doubts as to whether the enormous difficulties could be overcome by the traditional democratic methods and institutions. To some, the rise of Italian fascism since 1922 appeared to be an intriguing experiment, particularly since the Catholic Church, at least at the very beginning, did not oppose it.

In February 1932 de Valera's Party, Fianna Fáil (FF), emerged victorious from the general election. The new government replaced that of Cosgrave who had been determined throughout his term of office to fulfil the Anglo-Irish Treaty of 1922. There were also growing doubts as to Cosgrave's policy of free trade. Fianna Fail had been founded in May 1926 by de Valera who, having opposed the Treaty, gave up his policy of boycotting the Dáil Éireann in August 1927. This led to a split in the radical republican movement into a constitutional and a radical wing (the rest of Sinn Féin and the IRA).

De Valera pursued a policy of economic nationalism, the centrepiece being protective tariffs and far reaching autarchy. He stopped the agreed compensation payments, or annuities, to Britain. In retaliation Britain raised her tariffs for Irish goods considerably. A trade war broke out that was to last until 1938, inflicting untold damage on the Irish economy. De Valera also took other revolutionary measures such as abolishing the office of British Governor General to Ireland and the oath of allegiance to the British Crown. The Anglo-Irish Agreement was to be gradually dismantled, until in 1938 Irish-British relations were reformed, a diplomatic operation in which the British returned even so-called Treaty ports like Cobh, Berehaven and Lough Swilly to the Irish nation.

Sturm, in his 1984 thesis, has pointed out how many parallels there were between the circumstances of Germany and Ireland in the early Thirties. Such common features included a change of regime resulting from global economic collapse; heightened patriotism twinned with the belief of inherent superiority of national heritage and culture; a shared opposition to international treaties which were regarded as totally unjust i.e. Versailles and the Anglo-Irish Treaty, and their intended revision, sabotage or boycott of these bonds; the rejection of traditional Socialist and Liberal ideology, deemed to hold no relevance; the fledgling Soviet state seen as a menace, favouring the adoption of pure nationalism coupled with extensive state provision based on dictated social models; and the acceptance of an authoritarian style of leadership to counter the myriad of problems facing the two nation states.

Here, however, the parallels end because, in contrast to Germany, parliamentary democracy and its institutions were valued by the Irish as the precious result of a centuries-long struggle for independence. De Valera tended to practice an authoritarian style of governing, but he played by democratic rules and took democratic institutions into account. He considered Ireland firmly in the camp of Western democracies. His ideological base was not pure nationalism, less still racism, but a staunch Catholic faith.

The attitude of the Irish towards Germany before World War II was largely ambivalent. Barring a few convinced Irish fascists, who took their example from Mussolini rather than Hitler, the Irish had no sympathy with Nazism. Conscious of the economic plight, more than a few showed initial understanding and empathy for authoritarian regimes on the Continent. Amongst them must be included such prominent people as the Permanent Secretary at the Department of Foreign Affairs from 1922-46, Joseph Walsh, or William Butler Yeats, who in 1934 saw nothing wrong in accepting the Goethe Medal in Frankfurt under Nazi auspices. However, the more the true policy of the NSDAP towards the churches became apparent, the more Irish sympathy for Hitler's regime there vanished.

The Irish Blueshirts, of the National Guard and the Youth League, imitating similar fascist movements, won its recruits mainly from amongst the disenchanted farming community so badly hurt by de Valera's trade war with Britain. The Blueshirts' leader was General Eoin O'Duffy, a former Police Commissioner whom de Valera had dismissed. The Blueshirts were never anti-Church like the SS, SA or Hitler Youth. In 1936 the organisation was able to raise an Irish Brigade for Franco but this was considered a war against the atheistic communists. From then on, however, the Blueshirts lost their importance. The plan to form a 'Green Brigade' to fight on Hitler's side against the Bolsheviks was doomed from its inception.

While there were attitudes during the pre-war years that might strike outsiders as fascist, they can be explained by the extreme anti-communism of the time. Being a communist meant being an atheist and for the Irish, with the exception of some intellectuals, this was an alien concept. The unmistakable latent anti-semitism too, had a confessional rather than a racist background. Rather than a confrontational attitude, the Irish simply displayed a lack of sympathy or compassion for the Jewish people, coupled with a desire to make their own society as confessionally homogeneous as possible. Thus in political terms the pre-war period witnessed little rapprochement between Germany and Ireland. This was not true in economic terms. Due to the trade war with Britain the importance of Germany for the Irish economy grew. From 1932 onwards, the Irish Government tried to achieve a closer economic partnership. They offered, for instance, a deal connecting another power plant (on the Liffey) with a long-term supply of German coal. The German reaction was slow and reluctant at first. Once again, this time from the Nazi side, the thinking was that Germany need the friendship of Britain, an "Aryan germanic brother nation". The grand co-operation scheme with the Irish did not materialise. There were smaller projects such as providing assistance in building up the Irish sugar or turf energy industry. At the Shannon plant an additional turbine was installed.

Only the Third Reich's discovery that it lacked considerable amounts of foreign currency for its rearmament programme after 1935 led to a more dynamic approach. In January 1935 an Irish-German Trade Agreement was signed fixing the ratio of imports to exports at 3:1. This was enlarged to 2:1 in February 1936 and 3:2 at the end of that year. It was mainly agricultural products that Ireland was able to export. Between 1933 and 1938 Irish exports to Germany rose from £66,408 to £912,269, imports from Germany from £1.3 to £1.5 million. Nevertheless, Germany still trailed Britain.

There were few changes in this pre-war period as far as diplomatic relations were concerned. The German Ambassador von Dehn-Schmidt, in Dublin since 1923, was transferred as Ambassador to Bucharest in 1934. In Dublin he lived to see the first anti-Reich demonstrations against the Nazi treatment of the Jews on 28 March 1933. These were organised by Chief Rabbi Dr. Isaac Herzog, the father of Chaim Herzog, later to become President of Israel. Von Dehn-Schmidt, a career diplomat, reported the incident as was his duty. Whether during his eleven year stay in Ireland he was popular or not is debated by historians but neither judgement can be conclusively justified. He was certainly a man sympathetic to the nationalistic mood prevalent in Germany, which is not to say that he was necessarily a Nazi. He left a lasting mark through his friendship with the editor of the *Irish Times*, Robert Smyllie, an attentive, benevolent observer of the German scene who wrote two books, *A New Germany* in 1929, and *Germany Under Adolf Hitler* in 1936.

CR

Whatever von Dehn-Schmidt's performance, he did not deserve the treatment he was to receive at home. The story is characteristic of the Nazi period: when taking his leave in Dublin he followed the custom of paying a visit to the Dean of the Diplomatic Corps, the Papal Nuncio, who was an archbishop. As was customary at the time, the departing German Minister kissed the Nuncio's episcopal ring. A photo taken of this scene appeared in the Nazi Party's paper

'Völkischer Beobachter'. The Führer was outraged, as was the whole NSDAP. An official representative of the German nation had demeaned himself in front of the Pope's man, a behaviour unworthy of a true Aryan German. A press campaign started against von Dehn-Schmidt. Having been already installed as Ambassador in Bucharest, he was dismissed in February on a temporary basis and in November 1936 on a permanent one. Von Dehn-Schmidt died in July 1937 in Munich. His friend Robert Smyllie attended his funeral.

CR

The Irish Minister Binchy had already left the Irish Embassy in Berlin's Drake Straße 3 by 1932. On his return to Dublin he wrote a highly critical article on Hitler which was proof of his farsightedness and integrity. This made him persona non-grata with official Germany.

His successor did not arrive until the summer of 1933. Charles Bewley, the man who had tried his luck in 1922-23 with the Irish Office in Berlin, unlike Binchy, an unconditional admirer of the Third Reich. His reports were notoriously biased. In hindsight it seems astonishing that it took Dáil Éireann until 1937 to raise the question of his performance. Constant squabbling with his Government led to Bewley's recall and finally to his resignation in 1938. Bewley moved to Mussolini's Rome where he had been Ireland's representative at the Vatican in the Twenties. It was only in 1962 that Charles Bewley came to notice again by publishing a book on 'Hermann Göring and the Third Reich' with documents from Göring's family.

Bewley's succession was delayed and eventually overtaken by the outbreak of World War II. The Irish Government had designated Dr Joseph Thomas Kiernan, who was married to the singer Delia Murphy, the "blackbird of Irish ballads", for the position. However, since the request for an 'agrément', required formal approval from the British King as Head of the Commonwealth, this was out of the question once Britain found herself at war with Germany, which later prevented Hempel from being recalled or replaced. Kiernan would have to wait more than ten years before finally taking up his German post. Thus from 1938 to 1942, when he was granted home leave, the Chargé d'Affaire William Warnock represented Ireland in the Reich. From 1942 onwards Cornelius Cremin, previously Ireland's man in Vichy, held the position vacated by Warnock.

In Dublin, the successor to the unfortunate von Dehn-Schmidt was another career diplomat, Wilhelm von Kuhlmann. Upon leaving the ship at Cobh harbour he was met by a high official of the Irish Department of Foreign Affairs who greeted him with "Heil Hitler". The Irish Army band played not only the German national anthem "Deutschland, Deutschland über alles" but also the Nazi Party's song, the so-called Horst-Wessel-Lied. Without a hint of irony, the Irish Times reported the event the next day (on 25 October 1936) with a mention that "both German anthems, the old and the new one", had been heard.

The Minister's arrival was not free of incident. The German chancellery in Northumberland Road was smeared with the slogan 'Heraus mit Thälmann'. Thälmann, the leader of the German Communist Party, had been one of the first to be arrested by the Nazis; he was later killed. On the way to Aras an Uachtarán, the Irish President's mansion in the Phoenix Park, where he was to present his credentials, von Kuhlmann can hardly have missed the banners put up with the demand: "Free Thälmann! Down with Hitler!". Even von Kuhlmann's personal life in Dublin was not a happy one. His mother perished in a fire in his home in Cabinteely. He himself was ill most of the time and died after less than two years in Ireland.

He was succeeded by Dr Eduard Hempel. As he took up his assignment in 1937, he scarcely imagined that he was not to leave the Emerald Isle until twelve years later. Hempel, another career man, was no doubt a staunch patriot but not a militant Nazi. How he became head of a diplomatic mission, given that such postings required the seal of approval of the NSDAP, is unclear. According to one rumour, Mrs Hempel, being related to a holder of the Nazi 'Blood Order', had exploited this connection. She denied this after the war.

Right from the start Hempel's position was precarious. The war was to throw up all sorts of serious problems, making it impossible simply to sit back and perform 'bona figura', even had he so wished. There are, it must be said, no indications that Hempel attempted to test the limits of his loyalty to either Reich or Führer. He was in any case surrounded by watchers and informants from various Nazi circles: people from the Fichtebund (one of Goebbels' propaganda organisations), the 'Auslandsorganisation' (the Nazi Party's Foreign Department), the 'NSDAP Ortsgruppe' (the local Nazi Party cell), and the various German Secret Services. Worst of all, Hempel's Permanent Deputy at the Embassy, Thomson, was a member of the SS.

It is difficult to appreciate, retrospectively, how Germans living in Ireland could have been so utterly intoxicated by the Nazi ideology. The explanation seems to be that, because they were not directly exposed to the Nazi's daily meddling into people's private affairs at home, Germans abroad were particularly susceptible to nationalism. In the specific case of Ireland it has to be remembered too, that the 526 Germans living in Ireland in 1936 found themselves in an environment which was likewise highly nationalistic. Though disagreeing with basic features of Hitler's regime, many Irish people, out of profound dislike of the British and of Partition, felt that help from Germany against the "Auld Enemy" was not to be scoffed at. It is of little surprise that chauvinists in the German community were able to demonstrate their thinking openly and encountered sympathy from their Irish friends.

The local cell of the NSDAP which made Hempel's life difficult, was formed as early as May 1934, first under the leadership of Brase, then of Adolf Mahr, the Director of the Irish National Museum. It is interesting that at the same time a German Club was set up by representatives of the German business community (e.g. Müller-Dubrow-Siemens, Karl Krause-AEG). They met regularly at the Red Bank Restaurant in D'Olier Street in Dublin. The Party was not the be-all and the end-all of life for Germans living in Ireland. The Party cell had thirty one members, the German Club one hundred and twenty.

There was no major community of refugees, be they Jewish or political, in Ireland when the war started. Despite the fact that, according to the census of 1936 there were only 3,649 Irish citizens of Jewish faith in the country, de Valera's immigration policy was extremely restrictive. By mid-1939 not more than ninety Jewish refugees are reported to have been granted a temporary residence permit. In December 1939, some twenty 'christianised' i.e. baptised Jews from Hamburg were accepted. In 1940 another forty were allowed to follow. At first, most of them had difficulties in making ends meet. The majority were professional people whose diplomas were not automatically recognised. Some had to repeat their studies and exams. Amongst them was Dr R.A. Neumann from Berlin who was to become the medical adviser of most western European embassies in Dublin, a tradition his spouse continues to this very day. There was Professor Sachs, a scientist of great repute for his research on the determination of blood groups. In the liberal arts, Professor Levy, Dr Ernst Schyer and others were finally able to continue their work at Dublin's universities.

CR

On 11 September 1939, thirty-three men from the German community left Ireland for Germany, amongst them Dr Hellmut Clissmann of the DAAD-Academic Exchange Service, Dr Adolf Mahr of the National Museum, Müller-Dubrow from Siemens, the Celtic scholar Dr Ludwig Mühlhausen and the German University lecturers Helmut Bauersfeld and Hans Hartmann. At home they were either formally conscripted into the Army or given 'special assignments', mostly concerning Ireland. Clissmann was at first attached to the German Embassy in Copenhagen, then, as a soldier, to Military Intelligence (Canaris' *Abwehr*). Mahr obtained a position at the Foreign Ministry's Cultural Division. Mühlhausen became Professor of Celtic Studies, a leader of the Nazi Organisation for University Lecturers and finally 'Celtic expert in Northern France' for the SS. Bauersfeld and Hartmann were editors in the English speaking section of

Goebbels Radio Europe. Here Goebbels' Propaganda Ministry produced a regular radio programme for Britain and Ireland. Its most prominent foreign collaborators were William Joyce, alias Lord Haw-Haw, and the Irish author Francis Stuart. Stuart, having been a university lecturer in Berlin before the war, was in Ireland for a holiday when the war broke out, but managed to return to Berlin in January 1940 only with the help of Hempel. It was there that he thought himself able to best serve the Irish nationalist cause.

The other prominent figure at Goebbel's Radio Europe was William Joyce, a rather adventurous man. Born in New York, he joined Sir Oswald Mosley's British Union of Fascists, then founded a fascist party himself and finally went to Berlin to work for Goebbels. Joyce had acquired a British passport, under false pretences, a fact which was to be his downfall. The passport having expired in 1940, Joyce claimed American citizenship after the war. This, however, did not save him from the gallows. He had completed nine months of anti-British propaganda work while his British citizenship was valid, enough to have him sentenced to death for high treason and executed.

In Berlin the Third Reich based its information and assessment of Irish affairs mainly on the advice of this small community of returnees and expatriates. How one-sided this advice was and how wrongly informed the policy-makers in Berlin were is shown by a number of episodes. In February of 1939, for instance, a man called Oscar Pfaus from the NS-Fichtebund (founded by the Pan-Germans during World War I) turned up in Dublin to contact the IRA leader Séan Russell. Pfaus asked the Blueshirt leader O'Duffy to establish the contact, not knowing that O'Duffy and Russell were not on good terms. When Pfaus finally talked to Russell, Russell agreed to send Seamus (Jim) O'Donovan to Berlin with the mission to co-ordinate the IRA's policies with those of the Reich, a rather futile and naive undertaking. Despite Hempel's protest at home, the Fichtebund never stopped sending Nazi propaganda material to Irish sympathisers, albeit via London, thus compromising these people.

Many a reaction and attitude on the Irish side during those years can only be explained by ignorance of what was going on in the Reich and by profund hatred of all things British. For them the old slogan 'England's peril is Ireland's opportunity' was still valid. It must be noted, though, that the Irish media and most intellectuals were highly critical of the Reich and that initial pro-German attitudes in the rural areas vanished as the Nazi's treatment of the Church became known.

7. War Again

The Second World War opened a new chapter in Irish-German relations, albeit for the first time a highly political one. The principal concern of Berlin centred on Ireland's willingness and ability to stay neutral. Immediately after the outbreak of the war Foreign Minister Ribbentrop informed President de Valera, via Hempel, that the Reich was prepared to refrain from all hostile action against Irish territory provided Ireland observed "unimpeachable" neutrality. The expression "unimpeachable" did not please de Valera. He told Hempel that, due to Ireland's considerable economic dependence on Britain and the risk of a direct British intervention, the Irish Government could not but give certain considerations to Britain. There were three things he would not tolerate: any violation of Irish territory on land or sea, any exploitation of the anti-British nationalist movement in Ireland for anti-British actions and any hostile act against people on either side of the Northern Ireland border. This was duly reported by Hempel. De Valera was determined to keep neutrality at all costs. He emphatically declared in March 1941:

> *"It took hundreds of years of struggle to achieve Irish independence. We are determined not to let it get lost again."*

According to Hempel's analysis of the situation, shortly before and during the outbreak of the war, Ireland would have great difficulties in staying neutral. The extraordinary powers which the law of "emergency" conferred on de Valera did, however, improve his chance to maintain neutrality, against opposition in the Dail.

During the first months of the war the Irish greatly feared a British invasion designed to secure the flanks of their island. The use of such excellent natural harbours like

Cobh, (the return of which in 1937 Britain deeply regretted) was constantly requested by the British authorities. De Valera, however, stood firm. With the German campaign against England (Operation Sea Lion) the fear of occupation by the British receded. Irish minds were now concentrated on the threat of a German invasion, particularly after the shocking experience of Germany's occupation of neutral Belgium and the Netherlands.

Much of the residual goodwill towards Germany evaporated with these events. In August 1940, after urgent requests, Hempel finally received Ribbentrop's personal instructions. He was to tell de Valera that *"all competent German authorities have been given strict orders not to use Ireland as base for any action against Britain."*

ભ

This calmed Irish fears to some extent. At the beginning of 1940 the question of whether the Reich would include Ireland in her sea blockade of Britain became particularly pressing. The island's already strained supplies depended on this issue. Theoretically Berlin did not choose to do so. In actual fact the German navy repeatedly sank Irish ships, the first being the *Inver Liffey* as early as September 1939, followed by *the Munster* in February 1940. In April 1941 the Irish Embassy in Berlin had to protest against the sinking of three Irish freighters - the *Glencullen*, the *Glencree* and the *Edenvale*. In June 1942 the *City of Bremen* went down near the Scilly Isles. In May 1943 the *Irish Oak* was sunk. These are just a few examples from a long list of Irish ships destroyed by German torpedoes. At first there might have been the problem of proper identification, but once this question was solved the Reich had little excuse. In Berlin Irish protests were taken note of, apologies offered and promises given. But in the course of the war such unfortunate accidents happened again and again.

Irish-German relations were further strained by the accidental bombing of Irish territory, including towns, by German war planes. In the context of the 'Battle of Britain', which was meant to establish air superiority prior to an invasion of England, German bombers frequently took their route to the British west coast or to Ulster over the Irish Sea along the eastern coast of Ireland. During such flights, navigation errors, loss of orientation, and mistaken targets - sometimes the result of bad weather - were a common phenomenon. The fact that the Irish Government acceded to London's request to blackout Irish towns at least in the eastern part of the country (in order not to offer German planes an illuminated pathway to British Ulster) played a certain role.

The first such accident happened on 26 August 1940, in County Waterford, followed by many others in Drogheda, Knockroe, Curragh, Enniskerry, Terenure and elsewhere. The worst bombing occurred on 30 May 1941, at midnight in the Dublin suburb of Cabra, near the President's palace and the American Embassy. It resulted in 27 deaths, over 120 wounded, with 25 houses completely and 300 partially destroyed. Of course, the Irish Government did not fail to protest against such violations of international law. There is no evidence that even one of these unfortunate incidents was a deliberate and planned action. In each case the Reich's Government was highly embarrassed and pledged compensation immediately. A rather irritated German Foreign Office demanded from the Luftwaffe (Air Force) *"urgent clarification and future prevention of such mishaps"*. Hitler, Göring and von Ribbentrop were involved and discussed the affair. They gave strict orders for "no repetition", but to little avail. It was only Germany's defeat in the Battle of Britain and Hitler's turning towards Russia in the summer of 1941 that put an end to these most unfortunate infringements of Irish neutrality. From today's perspective it is astonishing to see the patience and fatalism with which most Irish people took these outrageous accidents at the time. Irish nationalist circles were even convinced that the German air force was victim of some devious technical device used by the British to divert the bombings to Ireland. This was however, technically impossible and therefore not a serious contention.

There was of course, the further question of the deliberate bombing of (British) Northern Ireland. The Primate of the Catholic Church of all Ireland, the Archbishop of

Armagh Cardinal MacRory, who was reputed to be pro-Axis, asked Hempel repeatedly to see to it that Armagh be spared the bombings. The same request was conveyed to Hempel by Secretary Joseph Walshe as far as Derry was concerned. Later in 1944, the eleven Irish, mainly religious, institutions in Rome were added to this list.

Another point of friction was espionage. The Germans were interested in weather data and information concerning Allied activities in Britain and Northern Ireland. It was the Embassy's task to report all relevant information received. It was, however, another matter to infiltrate agents into the country and to use them for the gathering of intelligence. The borderline seems to have been blurred occasionally. When in the context of the Battle of Britain, for instance, the arrival of an agent was announced to the Embassy, it was agreed that it would signal the start of a German invasion of England to the agents by putting up special flower boxes at the Chancellery windows.

In 1942 Hempel, having been informed by an Irish seaman who had returned from Britain, reported to Berlin that Canadian units were massing at the English South coast with the aim of an invasion at Dieppe. This operation did indeed take place on 19th August but failed miserably because the German side was too well prepared - probably due to Hempel's tip-off. As far as German spies in Ireland were concerned the Irish were very much in the picture at all times, not least because of co-operation with the British and American Secret Services, both of which functioned extremely well in Ireland.

In assessing the risks of espionage the basic German mistake at the time was twofold; firstly, they equated anti-British sentiment with pro-German feelings and thus over-estimated the strength and influence of the IRA. The advice given by those Irish friends residing in Berlin were responsible for this. The attempt was made repeatedly to try to exploit allegedly pro-German feelings and the expectations of Irish nationalists, i.e. the aim of some elements to force the British out of the six northern counties with the help of the Germans. De Valera had expressly warned against such tactics knowing that he could only maintain neutrality if Ireland did not become a region of anti-British agitation.

During the war de Valera came under increasing pressure from the Allies. David Gray, the American Ambassador, had direct access to the White House. He constantly demanded of de Valera that he abandon Ireland's neutrality citing German violations of Ireland's impartial status. The British Envoy to Ireland, Sir John Maffey, presented the Allied case in somewhat more diplomatic language. Even Cosgrave's Opposition party in the Dáil was in favour of the Allies' request. It was therefore a most precarious situation in which Hempel, eager to assist de Valera in his policy of neutrality, found himself. His fear that covert activities by German agents could be considered a provocation by the Allies and could lead to Allied intervention in Ireland, was not without some justification. In 1942 the situation was such that the German Embassy took the precautionary measure of destroying all confidential files including those of the NSDAP Ortsgruppe.

The risk of Ireland being occupied by the Allies again became very acute after America's entry into the war and the establishment of American bases in Northern Ireland. With hindsight it could be argued that the possibility of setting up such bases in Ulster saved the Irish Republic. In the absence of such an opportunity, Allied preparations for the invasion of the Continent might well have led to an occupation of the Irish Republic.

Berlin reacted to the risk of an Allied occupation of Ireland with a decision to make de Valera an offer of military assistance. As early as 1940 a special section had been established in the German Foreign Office which, under the direction of SS-Standartenführer Veesemeyer, was to support the war effort by planning subversive actions abroad. Ireland, a relatively small fish, was one of the countries targeted, although major operations were directed towards Eastern Europe. Veesemeyer's advisors on Ireland convinced him that in the event of an Allied occupation de Valera, closing ranks with the IRA, would not hesitate to defend the country to the last drop of blood.

In January 1942 Dr Hellmut Clissmann, until 1939 the German Academic Exchange Service's man in Dublin, who was seconded to Veesemeyer from Canaris' Military Intelligence, undertook a mission to Madrid to contact the Irish Ambassador to Spain, Leopold Kerney. Kerney was reputed to be a close friend of de Valera and of right wing convictions. Asked his opinion, he confirmed to Clissmann his assumptions and predicted that, once confronted with an Allied invasion, de Valera would not only put his differences with the IRA aside but also appeal to the Reich for assistance. Hempel was instructed to sound out de Valera's response and to ask whether in such an event the Irish Government would at least accept German arms. To the disappointment of Hempel and Berlin, de Valera did not reply to any such suggestion but simply changed the subject.

In Berlin the 'experts' knew better. They were determined to be prepared for the moment when their assistance would be required. Following a number of meetings with Ribbentrop, who no doubt informed the Führer, it was decided to have one SS-Standartenführer Schellenberg form a group of 120 SS men who would be prepared for such an event. Hempel's reports of Irish non-reaction made an impact in the end. Veesemeyer abandoned this grand scheme, reduced the number to between ten and twelve men and provided them with a revised objective: *"to mobilise and support the existing Irish resistance forces and to establish a faultless information system."*

છ

The actual German espionage operations in Ireland came to resemble a poor farce. The Goertz case was to become a source of constant trouble for the Embassy. The Canaris man Dr Herman Goertz, having been parachuted into Meath on 6 May 1940, managed to join Francis Stuart's wife Iseult, daughter of Maud Gonne, in the Wicklow Mountains, and subsequently other friends, in hiding for some months. Iseult Stuart was later arrested, but acquitted and released. Goertz's other contact, the Irish informant Held, whose transmitter was discovered, was less fortunate: he was sentenced to five years' imprisonment. It was with Held that the Irish authorities found 'Plan Kathleen' which, in the event of an invasion of England, foresaw a German landing in Derry with assistance from the IRA. It is by no means clear who conceived this plan, be it the Germans or the IRA. Goertz succeeded for some time to get radio messages through to Germany. One wonders though what he had to report.

Goertz's mission was clearly defined: to prepare acts of sabotage against Britain, to carry them out as far as possible with the help of the IRA, but under no circumstances to taint the Irish Government with such actions. This of course, was the squaring of the circle and exactly what de Valera had warned against. Goertz's activities proved quite fruitless, serving only as a source of irritation for Germany and Ireland alike. Goertz himself, who had been in a British prison for espionage before the war, was soon frustrated and felt left in the lurch, in both financial and political terms. Hempel reported Goertz being seriously depressed after two vain attempts to leave Ireland by boat. Even Veesemeyer and the Under-Secretary in the German Foreign Office, Woermann, called Goertz a "Belastung" or nuisance. At the end of 1941 Goertz was arrested, imprisoned and later interned.

Another agent was the sixty year old former pro-fessional boxer Weber-Drohl who in March 1940 had come as a money courier for the IRA. Having been arrested he too, for reasons of ill health, was interned. To the same tragi-comic cast belonged Gartner, Tributh and Obed (two of South African and one of Indian nationality) who in July 1940 landed on the Irish south coast. It is said that, having been thoroughly prepared for their mission, they were immediately arrested after asking a local bus driver in perfect Gaelic what the name of the next village was. Also, all three had only Irish money with continual serial numbers!

Other agents like Walter Simon, alias Karl Anderson, Willy Preetz, alias Paddy Mitchell were also quickly discovered and arrested, as were Günter Schulz alias Hans Marschner, Van Loon and Werner Umland. The same fate met two Irishmen who, allegedly in the service of the German

Navy, were parachuted into Kilkee in County Limerick as late as December 1943 to hand over transmitters to the IRA.

Plans to channel IRA activists into Ireland from Germany were less ridiculous but no more successful. The idea was to bring the leaders of the right and of the left wing of the IRA together, smuggle them into Ireland and have them operate against the British from there. In August 1940 a German submarine brought the right wing IRA leader Sean Russell from the USA to Germany to meet the left leaning IRA representative Frank Ryan. Both were put on another submarine, but on the voyage Sean Russell died of a perforated gastric ulcer 100 miles off the coast of Galway. Frank Ryan returned to Germany. All hope was now centred on him. Ryan, who had fought in the Spanish civil war on the republican side, was sentenced to death by Franco and finally released only on German intervention. He was now the Reich's "most important Irishman" and was personally looked after by Veesemeyer. But on 13th January 1943, shortly before he was to become operative in Ireland, he suffered a stroke and was admitted to the Berlin Charité Hospital. He later died of pneumonia in a clinic near Dresden.

Another attempt was made in 1942 to land German agents by amphibious planes in order to provide the IRA with money and transmitters. There were several meetings on the subject between Veesemeyer and Ribbentrop at such places as Zagreb and Schloß Fuschl at Salzburg. Ribbentrop was rather sceptical and held back. In the end all these plans failed for the simple reason that the German Navy refused to put amphibious planes at Veesemeyer's disposal.

When planning the invasion of England General Leonhard Kaupisch, Commander of the Fourth and the Seventh Army Corps in France, gave orders to draw up a plan for the invasion of Ireland. There existed an "Operation Green" plan which envisaged the formation of a bridgehead stretching from Gorey, Mount Leinster and Thomastown to Clonmel and Dungarvan which would secure the flanks of potential German operations in England.

This plan was a prime example of numerous such schemes where it cannot be established whether they were real, part of military 'occupational therapy' or simply intended to confuse the enemy.

Finally the Third Reich again attempted to form an Irish Brigade from British PoWs of Irish descent. The 'Ireland Specialists' in Berlin had obviously learned nothing from Casement's failure in World War I. A special camp was installed at Friesack near Brandenburg, but all the efforts made to indoctrinate and turn the 'Irish' PoWs around were futile.

CR

Another problematic point in Irish-German relations during the war was the question of the German internees in Ireland. Although there existed full diplomatic relations with the Third Reich, thus entitling German and Irish nationals to live freely in each others countries, it was for Ireland quite within international law to arrest and intern any military personnel entering the island. Thus during the course of the war more than 250 Germans were interned, mostly in the Curragh Camp in Country Kildare. Except for those who were considered agents or spies, all of them were either shipwrecked sailors or pilots landing due to emergency.

The first German plane crashed as early as August 20th, 1940, at Mount Brandon on the Dingle peninsula. Among those rescued was Lieutenant First Class Kurt Mollenhauer who was to become Chief Officer at the Curragh Camp for more than four years. A dozen further crashes or emergency landings followed until 1944.

On 29 December 1943, in a uniquely selfless and heroic act, the crew of the 335 ton Irish freighter *Kerlogue* rescued 168 shipwrecked Germans whose three ships had been sunk between Brest and St. Nazaire. The captain of the Kerlogue showed enormous courage not only by risking his own and his men's lives but also by ignoring both the general instruction to get a British 'Navicert' at Fishguard before returning home and the specific British demand to turn the Germans over to them. By the time the British Representative Sir John Maffey protested in Dublin it was too late -

the Germans were already at the Curragh. There, in March 1945, 48 crew members of a German submarine, tor-pedoed off the Cork coast, joined the others.

The internees at the Curragh were generally very well treated. Free to leave the camp frequently, they occupied themselves by doing gardening, playing tennis in nearby Newbridge, visiting local pubs, dancing and even visiting cafés in Dublin. More than a few formed friendships with Irish girls, of whom at least five married their German fiancés at the end of the war. Of course, provisions could not be better than with the Irish themselves who, exposed to a de facto embargo, were suffering from all kinds of shortages.

Homesickness, the monotony of camp life and the unavoidable friction between inmates led constantly to frustration, impatience and boredom. There were attempts at escape (one actually succeeded in getting as far as England), complaints and problems of discipline. The Embassy did its best to mediate and to make the Irish authorities alleviate the internment conditions. It succeeded even in persuading them to let some of the internees stay in Dublin and attend university courses.

At the end of the war there were 266 people due for repatriation. Nobody was forced to return to what had by then become the Soviet Occupied Zone of Germany. Only 138 volunteered to go home. Fifty asked to be allowed to stay but were refused. With the exception of a handful who had married Irish girls all German military personnel left the Emerald Isle. Not so the seven agents who were granted formal asylum. Van Loon and Schultz, the man who once escaped from Mountjoy prison, also married Irish women and established rights of residence in Ireland.

When in April 1947 the War Crimes trials began in Germany the Allies asked to extradite the agents, amongst them Goertz. Having been in a British prison for espionage before the war, he panicked. In vain he tried to get to South America. Shortly before his extradition was to take place, he took his own life in Dublin Castle's Aliens Registration Office, by taking poison. Between the summer of 1945 and the spring of 1947 Goertz had been working tirelessly to organise the "Save the German Children" campaign.

A final act of heroism took place months after the end of the war, as late as January 1946. A group of German PoWs, acting with the French who were deployed in mine sweeping operations, got hold of a mine sweeper and escaped from St. Nazaire to Ireland. On landing at Kinsale, County Cork, they were enthusiastically received and very well cared for by the local population of the charming harbour town. However, after a few days under French and British pressure, the Irish Government felt obliged to return crew and ship to France.

CR

Yet another major concern during the war was the Embassy's channels of communication with Berlin. The Embassy, in possession of a covert wireless transmitter, was in contact with Berlin at first directly until mid-1941, and then indirectly via the German Embassy in Bern, Switzerland. The unauthorised transmitter, however, had been discovered by Irish and British intelligence as early as January 1940. From this point on the Allies kept reminding the Irish Government of this "irregularity" by requesting the closure of the German delegation. The transmitter became a real bone of contention. As the only possibility of a courier service was via London, this understandably being considered unsafe, the German Embassy depended upon this transmitter more than anything else.

Regular telegraphic connections, again via London, were in time of war extremely unreliable and slow. The Irish Government on the other hand, finding itself under constant pressure from the British and later the Americans, had to do something about the matter. At first Hempel was asked to refrain from using it. He assured Secretary Joseph Walshe that he would do so only in case of emergency. But how was this to be controlled?

The matter was left in limbo for quite some time. In October 1942 the evidence of the Embassy's usage of the transmitter, as presented by the Allies, was so overwhelming that Walshe had to issue a warning of serious action against the German Embassy. It took until December 1943, however, for de Valera to present Hempel with an ultimatum to hand the transmitter over. Hempel, unable to stall any longer, sent his last report via Bern on 17 December 1943. In it he conveyed de Valera's Christmas Message to the Irish people. Then, shortly before Christmas Eve, the transmitter was locked up jointly by Hempel and Walshe in a bank safe, with each man being given one of the two keys.

The impossibility for Berlin of looking after its Dublin mission soon led to other difficulties, particularly in the supply of money, which also affected payments to the internees. The delegation, being literally broke, even went to court to call in the debts owed to German creditors by Irish debtors, but to no avail. On de Valera's initiative the Embassy was given a loan. It was not until February 1st, 1945, that an Irish-German agreement on German war damages was finalised, salvaging the embarrassing situation. The Irish Government was now entitled to call in debts from Irish debtors and put the money in a special account from which the costs of the German Embassy, the German internees and the war damages were to be paid. The latter had been deliberately under-valued at only £40,000. Later, in 1953, the actual costs were put at almost £500,000.

A last widely publicised episode of May 1945 must also be noted. After Hitler's suicide on April 30th, 1945, he being in a formal sense the Head of State with which Ireland had diplomatic relations, the Embassy followed international practice by displaying a book of condolences. On May 2nd, de Valera, Joseph Walshe and Michael McDunphy, President Douglas Hyde's Secretary, went to sign the book. By doing this not at the Chancellery but at Hempel's residence they wanted to express their special respect for the German Minister himself. The formal gesture, although in conformity with international custom, led to uproar in the British and American media. To this very day de Valera's decision in this respect is highly controversial.

For the German nationals in Ireland the first few months of 1945 were a time of great uncertainty over whether the Irish would follow the example of many hitherto neutral States which, in order to court the favour of the probable victors, entered war against the Axis at the eleventh hour. De Valera did nothing of the sort. Even before Germany's capitulation the American Ambassador Gray requested the closure of the German legation and the extradition of its files and archives. De Valera refused. Sir John Maffey also disagreed with Gray. The British Foreign Minister Anthony Eden considered the action useless, since everything important would have been destroyed anyway. Churchill, however, supported Gray's request and on the 10th of May 1945, the inevitable came to pass - the keys of the German Embassy were handed over not to the Irish but to Gray. Later at an auction in Belfast all movable objects of the Embassy were sold for £1,700. The building of the Chancellery in Northumberland Road, having been given to the British, also went up for sale.

The members of the German Embassy retired to their private life and awaited repatriation. De Valera granted asylum to Hempel whom he had grown to respect. Hempel, without job or income (his employer, the Reich, had ceased to exist), tried to make ends meet. It is said that he even received some material support from de Valera (Mrs Hempel proved to be a gifted baker and provided shops and friends with German cakes and biscuits). It was with the help of his former British colleague Sir John Maffey who, always the gentleman, had partially been educated in Germany, that Hempel finally, after four years of precarious existence in Ireland, managed to return to Bonn in 1949 where the Ministry gave him the same job he had held before he left in 1936. After only two years of active service he retired and died at the age of 85 on 12 November 1972 in Freiburg. There was no official representation at his funeral.

8. Post-war Years

In the years immediately after the Second World War Irish-German ties underwent a revival with a series of generous humanitarian actions on the part of the Irish. As so often before and after they sided with the 'underdog'. Besides the important donations such as money and foodstuffs given to Germans in dire need it was, above all, Ireland's co-operation in international aid organisations like UNWRA involving numerous Irish nurses and doctors which was so impressive. Next to the Irish Red Cross, the Catholic aid organisations were particularly active in reviving the old contacts between the Churches of both countries.

The "Save the German Children" campaign, founded by Dr Kathleen Murphy, among others, remains particularly well remembered. To try to bring needy German children, many of whom were orphans, over to Ireland in that period after 1945 proved extremely difficult and required a great deal of perseverance. Germany's infrastructure had broken down completely and there was a lot of opposition and lack of goodwill on the part of the occupation forces. It was only after more than a year's effort that the Irish fund managers were able to get 190 German children to come to Ireland, 134 of them being immediately integrated into Irish families. Another 126 arrived in November 1946 so that the total number in April 1947 reached 418, and 518 by 1948. Donations for the Fund totalled 1.3 million Deutschmarks.

At first the children were meant to stay for three years. Many a family asked to keep them for good or to adopt them. There were emotionally difficult moments. In the end fifty children were allowed to remain with their Irish foster parents. As a token of gratitude a bronze fountain by the German sculptor Josef Wackerle (called the 'Nornenbrunnen') was donated by Federal President Theodor Heuß and put up in St Stephen's Green Park in Dublin in 1954.

The campaign was also responsible for the setting up of a German school in Dublin. Out of modest beginnings grew the highly regarded educational establishment of St Kilian's German School, which with a special emphasis on German language has led hundreds of mostly Irish children right up to their Leaving Certificate.

The start of official relations between the two countries had to wait another couple of years. Though founded in 1948, the Federal Republic did not possess full sovereignty and was at first unable to enter into diplomatic relations with other states. Ireland was one of the first to express a wish to establish some sort of relations. In early 1951 the Irish special envoy John A. Belton had talks with Permanent Secretary Haas of Chancellor Adenauer's office. They agreed to establish at least consular links. Belton made it clear that he did not want to request any sort of approval by the Allied High Commissioners.

On 18 January 1951, the request for a post of Consul General for Dublin was placed on the order of business in the Bundestag (Parliament). To the dismay of the officials Parliament did not approve a Consulate First, but only Second Class. The Government did not give in initially, and only on the 3 February, the matter was once again on the agenda and, given the explanation that otherwise the Dublin mission would not be reinstated to its pre-war status, the Bundestag revised its decision. The fact that there was a well-known candidate for the post waiting in the wings might have been a deciding factor. On 27 January 1951, Bonn's main newspaper, the General-Anzeiger, leaked a story that Geheimrat Dr. Katzenberger, the Director of the Bundesrat and former spokesman of North Rhine-Westphalia's Prime Minister Arnold, had been chosen to go to Dublin. Having served as Secretary General of the Catholic Centre Party (Zentrum) during the Weimar Republic, and for a short while in the Foreign Ministry after 1932, he was dismissed by the Nazis on the grounds of "lack of political reliability".

Belton, being up for presentation of credentials to President Heuß on 11 June and thinking of reciprocity, became impatient with what he considered the extremely slow handling of Katzenberger's dispatch. He was told however, that the Allied High Commissioners were about to change the rules and give the Federal Government the right to have diplomatic relations. Thus it was finally possible to accredit Katzenberger not as Consul but as Minister Plenipotentiary.

The first members of the future Embassy, having arrived in Dublin in June 1951, took temporary residence at the Parkside Hotel in Dublin's North Circular Road and arranged the essentials for setting up a diplomatic mission. In this they were assisted by the Irish Chief of Protocol, the Swiss Ambassador and the law firm of Arthur Cox and Partners. On 12 July 1951 Katzenberger, staying at the Shelbourne Hotel, handed over his credentials to President Séan O'Kelly.

In 1955 Belton was replaced by Dr. Thomas Joseph (Tom) Kiernan, the man who twelve years earlier had been meant to take over from Bewley but had been prevented from doing so by the war (or rather the British King). Both Katzenberger and Kiernan retired in 1956. The first prominent Irish visitor to Bonn after the war was Tánaiste Séan Lemass as Minister of Industry and Commerce in August 1952. What was left over from the war was easily dealt with. With reference to the financial agreement of February 1945, all claims were compensated. The net surplus of what the Irish Government had collected from Irish debtors and paid out from those special accounts amounted to £51,646. German war damages were fixed at £446,820. Bonn did not hesitate to settle the balance of £395,174 immediately. A whole new chapter of friendly and smooth relations between the two Governments and, more important still, between the two peoples was opened.

It was with some hesitation that after the war and their economic recovery the first Germans came to discover the mysterious Emerald Isle. The frosty climate of the Cold War being fought right in the middle of Germany itself, coupled with the even graver events in Budapest and Prague and then, of course, the erection of the Berlin Wall in 1961 - these crises turned many a German away from the Continent and towards Ireland, with its enviable location on Europe's Western periphery. Given the very real fear that the Soviets might well take over the small Federal Republic, there was something to be said for taking refuge in the relative security of Ireland. Thus after 1961 came the first wave of investments in Ireland by German business people and farmers, who bought manor houses, cottages or farms, of which there was no dearth on the Irish property market for reasonable prices, or started manufacturing goods in Ireland.

But even before that there were some few Germans who, traumatised and victimised by the events of the war, wanted to get away from it all. Probably the first was Prince Ernst Heinrich of Saxony, the youngest of three sons of the former King of Saxony, Friedrich August III of the House of Wettin. It is most remarkable how as early as 1947 he succeeded in settling in Ireland long before the establishment of the Federal Republic: Prince Ernst, an agronomist, having been entrusted with the administration of the House of Wettin, left the family castle of Moritzburg near Dresden very late in the war, only after Dresden's air raid destruction (February 13th, 1945), and after the Russians had already occupied nearby Görlitz. By rather adventurous means and with almost no belongings he reached the town of Sigmaringen where his sister, the Princess of Hohenzollern-Sigmaringen, offered him shelter. His elder brother Christian, the Markgraf of Meißen, was accommodated by the Duke of Württemberg.

Shortly after his arrival the French Armed Forces occupied Sigmaringen and French officers of nobility came into contact with the princes. It was thus that they learned of a treasure, one of the few things Prince Ernst Heinrich had been able to salvage out of the rubble of Dresden: the crown of Louis IX, the famous thirteenth century French King (1226-70). The crown had been in Wettiner possession for some time and had miraculously survived Dresden's bombardment in a safe which - after the raids - hung high up in the wall of Dresden City Castle and had to be taken down by the fire brigade at the very last moment before the Russians arrived.

The French Government, anxious to get the crown, immediately started negotiations with the two Saxon princes. In exchange for the crown the French offered not only financial compensation but also assistance of any kind in the princes' plans to start a new life. For Prince Ernst Heinrich who had lost everything in the Soviet Zone both were of great importance. Faced with the seemingly hopeless situation of Germany in 1946 the Prince expressed his wish to settle in Ireland as a farmer. This was not an easy thing to realise, as Germans were neither allowed to leave the Occupation Zones they were in nor to settle in foreign lands without Allied permission nor to possess foreign currency. The French Government contacted the Irish Government and finally succeeded in acquiring for the prince not only an Irish residence permit but also the licence to buy land in Ireland. With French financial help Prince Ernst Heinrich, with his wife and two sons, was thus able to move to Ireland where he bought a dairy farm in County Westmeath. Earlier on, in a most impressive ceremony at the Saint Chapel in Paris, the two Wettiner princes had handed over Louis IX's crown. Prince Ernst Heinrich of Saxony died in Westmeath in 1971 at the age of seventy-four.

The legacy of Heinrich Böll's *Irish Diary* written in 1954-55 continues to be felt to this day. It was this book, the Nobel Prize Winner's best-seller of 1957, that truly brought Ireland into German popular consciousness as an irresistible place to visit, initiating the love affair that so many Germans have had and continue to have with Ireland. In addition, the beneficial effects of vastly improved means of transportation and communication should not be overlooked either.

Official Ireland's attitude to Böll's depiction of the country as a haven of romantic backwardness was understandably cool at first, only to thaw somewhat at the realisation that Böll had generated enormous German enthusiasm for what was soon a country "en route to modernity". Böll himself, writing in *"Thirteen Years Later"*, conceded that the 1960s had already ushered in enormous changes:

"It's as if Ireland in 1954 and 1955 offered us a glimpse of that historic moment when it began to skip a century and a half and make up for a further five."

He did not say for sure whether he still believed what he had said in the mid Fifties: *"that the Irish live closer to Heaven than other Europeans".* He must have felt that way himself in his cottage in Dugort on Achill Island, Co. Mayo.

Professor Kuno Meyer

Sir Roger Casement

R.M. Smyllie and Col. Fritz Brase

Commandant F.C. Sauerzweig

Commandant Fitzmaurice, Baron von Hünefeld, Kapitän Köhl

Francis Stuart

Clockwise from top left:
Dr. Georg von Dehn-Schmidt, Ambassador 1923 - 1934,
Wilhelm von Kuhlmann, Ambassador 1934 - 1937,
Dr. Hermann Katzenberger, Ambassador 1951 - 1956,
Dr. Edward Hempel, Ambassador 1937 - 1945

Ernst Heinrich, Prince of Saxony

Deutschland und Irland

1000 Jahre gemeinsamer Geschichte

Martin Elsasser

Inhaltsverzeichnis

Vorwort

Den deutschen Freunden Irlands, und den irischen Freunden Deutschlands möchte ich zeigen, wann und wie die beiden Völker miteinander in Berührung gekommen sind und wie sie sich gegenseitig beeinflußt haben. Der Leser wird feststellen, daß nicht so sehr offizielle Beziehungen, sondern Menschen, Iren und Deutsche, die gemeinsame Geschichte geprägt haben.

Das Buch ist eine hoffentlich unterhaltsame Zusammenfassung, die - ohne Anspruch auf akademische Vollständigkeit zu erheben - dem Leser ersparen will, die zahl- und umfangreichen Monographien zu studieren, die zu fast jedem Aspekt des deutsch - irischen Verhältnisses geschrieben worden sind.

Wer sich mit einzelnen Themen näher befassen möchte, findet am Ende des Buches eine Literaturauswahl.

Ich danke allen, insbesondere Frau Traudl Tscher-ning, die mir bei der Redaktion des Textes geholfen haben.

Martin Elsasser, Dublin, im Juni 1997

1. Keltische Ahnen, irische Heilige

Die Gemeinsamkeit beginnt mit den Kelten: nicht nur Irland, auch deutsche Lande haben einen keltischen Hintergrund. Weite Teile Deutschlands, Österreichs und Böhmens waren von Kelten besiedelt. Erst in der Zeit der Völkerwanderung des 4. und 5. Jahrhunderts n.Chr. wurden sie von germanischen Stämmen absorbiert oder in oft höher gelegene, unfruchtbarere Bergregionen abgedrängt, wo sie allmählich ihre keltische Identität verloren. Viele archäologische Funde zeugen von dem hohen Entwicklungsstand der Kelten im deutschsprachigen Raum. Sie stammen aus der jüngeren Urnenfelderzeit (10.-8. Jh. v.Chr.), der Hallstattzeit (8.-5. Jh. v.Chr.) und der La Tènezeit (5.-1. Jh. v.Chr.).

Am eindrucksvollsten zeigen die Ausgrabungen im bayerischen Manching die keltische Oppida-Zivilisation des zweiten und ersten Jahrhunderts v.Chr., die erst mit den römischen oder den germanischen Eroberungen unterging. Die Forschung geht davon aus, daß in Manching auf einer Fläche von 380 Hektar fast 10000 Kelten in einer straff organisierten, städtischen Kultur zusammengelebt haben.

Fast alle einsilbigen Namen der Flüsse in Deutschland sind keltischen Ursprungs: Ruhr, Rhein, Lahn, Main sind Beispiele. Ebenso gehen Neckar und Isar auf keltische Worte zurück. Selbst in dem Begriff 'deutsch' sehen einige eine Verwandtschaft mit dem keltischen 'tuath' für 'völkisch'.

Allerdings muß an dieser Stelle auch gesagt werden, daß diejenigen Kelten (von Ptolemäus *Ierni/Iverni* genannt und davon abgeleitet auch der lateinische Name *Hibernia*), die sich schließlich auf der irischen Insel ansiedelten, mit größter Wahrscheinlichkeit nicht aus dem Raum kamen, der jetzt deutschsprachig ist. Woher, wann und welche Kelten nach Irland gelangten, ist ungewiß. Dennoch können viele

Deutsche davon ausgehen, daß auch in ihren Adern keltisches Blut (mit)fließt.

Die ersten historisch dokumentierten Kontakte fallen in die Zeit der Christianisierung der Stämme, die damals in deutschen Landen wohnten. Nach der Bekehrung der Iren durch den Heiligen Patrick (ab 432) nahm sie ihren Ausgang von Irland und zielte zunächst auf das benachbarte Britannien. Dort gründete der Ire St.Columba (irisch: *Columcille*) 563 n.Chr. auf der (jetzt) schottischen Hebrideninsel Iona ein Kloster. Es war nicht diese geographische Tatsache, die dafür verantwortlich ist, daß auf dem europäischen Kontinent im ganzen Mittelalter die Iren fälschlicherweise Schotten genannt worden sind. Davor hatten schon die Römer die Iren als *scoti* bezeichnet. Sie gingen davon aus, daß Schottland und Irland (Länder, die sie nie eroberten) von den gleichen Stämmen bewohnt waren. Die Bezeichnung 'scoti' hielt sich, solange die lateinische Sprache lingua franca war, also bis zum Beginn der Neuzeit.

Die missionarische Tätigkeit irischer Mönche auf dem europäischen Kontinent setzte um 600 n.Chr. ein. Zwei Motive bewogen die Iren des 6. und 7. Jahrhunderts: *"peregrinatio pro amore dei"* ('die Wanderschaft aus Liebe zu Gott'; Lk.9,23) und der biblische Auftrag *"docete omnes gentes"* ('allen Völkern das Evangelium zu verkünden'; Math.28,19).

Vom nordirischen Bangor aus machte sich so ein Schüler Columbas, der sich Columbanus (543-615) nannte, mit 12 Gefährten ins westliche Reich der Franken (Frankreich) auf. Dort gründete er zuerst eine größere Klosteranlage in Luxeuil und danach noch weitere monastische Siedlungen. Im Jahre 610 aus Frankreich vertrieben, begab er sich zu den Langobarden nach Italien, wo er sich endgültig in Bobbio niederließ. Auf dem Wege dorthin machte er in der heutigen Schweiz und in Österreich halt und wies seine Begleiter an, zu bleiben und Missionsstationen einzurichten: so gründeten der Heilige Gallus 612 St. Gallen und ein weiterer Ire Bregenz.

Eine zweite Welle irischer Missionare folgte und breitete sich nicht nur in das westliche, sondern auch in das östliche Frankenreich aus. In Bayern erinnern daran noch die Namen der Heiligen Declanus, Marinus und Annianus, die in der ersten Hälfte des 7. Jahrhunderts von Freising und vom Irschenberg aus missionierten.

Am nachhaltigsten und populärsten bleibt das Andenken an die Heiligen Kilian (irisch: *Kilena*), Colman und Totnan im Würzburger Raum bewahrt, wo alle drei im Jahre 689 den Märtyrertod erlitten haben sollen. Wie bedeutend Kilian war, zeigt der liturgische Kalender der damaligen Frankenkönige. Er kennt nur zwei Heilige aus dem deutschsprachigen rechtsrheinischen Reich: Bonifaz und Kilian. Im Martyrologium des Mönches Beda Venerabilis (ca. 850) heißt es unter dem 8. Juli: *"An eben diesem Tag wurde der Bischof Kilian im Kastrum Wirziburg mit seinen Gefährten unter Herzog Gozbert gemartert."*

Es gibt zwar keine schriftlichen Zeugnisse dieser drei Märtyrer, und was überliefert ist, stammt aus zwei Handschriften des 9. Jahrhunderts, der *passio Kiliani minor* und der *passio maior*. Die außerordentlich lang zurückgehende Tradition, die an Kilian glaubt, spricht jedoch für seine historische Existenz; immerhin ließ bereits 752 - zur Zeit König Pippins und des Heiligen Bonifaz - Burkard, der erste Bischof von Würzburg, Gebeine, die den Märtyrern zugeschrieben werden, zur Ehre der Altäre erheben. Der damalige Papst Zacharias hatte seine Zustimmung gegeben. Im Jahre 788 wurden diese Reliquien in Gegenwart Karls des Großen feierlich in den neu erbauten Würzburger Salvatordom überführt.

Bemerkenswert ist die angebliche Ursache des Märtyrertodes, in der eine Parallele zum Schicksal Johannes des Täufers gesehen wurde. St. Kilian wird nachgesagt, mit Herzog Gozbert von Wircibur [Würzburg] wegen einer Frage des Eherechts in Konflikt geraten zu sein. Das kirchliche Recht, das sich auf Lev. 18,16 berief und für das sich Kilian energisch einsetzte, verbot die Ehe zwischen Verschwägerten, während das fränkische Recht das nicht tat. Der Fürst ließ sich jedoch nicht davon abbringen, nach dem Tod seines Bruders seine Schwägerin Geilana zu heiraten. Ob Geilana beim Tod ihres Gatten etwas nachgeholfen hatte, ist nicht bekannt, jedenfalls soll sie sich durch Kilians öffentlichen Widerspruch erheblich irritiert gefühlt und seine Ermordung angeordnet haben.

CR

Kilian und seine Mannen waren nicht die einzigen irischen Missionare im Deutschland des 7. und 8. Jahrhunderts. Aus dieser Zeit ist der Ire Dobdagrecus als Abt des Klosters Chiemsee überliefert. Neben dem Heiligen Erhard gelten auch Emeran und Korbinian (beide im Freisinger Raum tätig) als Iren, ebenso wie Virgil (irisch: *Fergil*), der 748 vom Bayern-Herzog Odilo beauftragt wurde, das Bistum Salzburg aufzubauen. Der Heilige Albert, ein Gefährte Erhards und auch ein Ire, wird in seiner *Vita* von 1150 als ehemaliger Bischof von Cashel bezeichnet. Sicher ist, daß er im 7. Jahrhundert in Regensburg gestorben ist. Auf den irischen Einsiedler Alto geht Altomünster zurück. Im Kloster Rheinau bei Schaffhausen ließ sich der Ire Findan in eine Zelle einmauern. Elf irische Mönche, die mit dem Angelsachsen Willibrord gekommen waren, missionierten in Friesland, Fridolin bei den Allemannen. Dissibold, dessen Lebensgeschichte Hildegard von Bingen 1170 geschrieben hat, war zusammen mit den irischen Gefährten Clement, Griswald, Salust in der Trierer und Mainzer Gegend tätig. Im späten Mittelalter wurden im deutschsprachigen Raum nachweislich über 100 irische Missionare als Heilige verehrt.

Daß wir noch heute in vielen deutschen Städten 'Schottenkirchen' oder 'Schottenklöster' finden, ist nicht verwunderlich, da sie alle auf Gründungen irischer Mönche zurückgehen. Aber nicht nur die mönchische Frömmigkeit, sondern auch die Gelehrsamkeit der Iren galt als beispielhaft. Handschriften („*libri Scotice scripti*"), dem berühmten *Book of Kells* vergleichbar, befinden sich in vielen alten deutschen Bibliotheken. Am bekanntesten ist ein Manuskript der Paulusbriefe mit zahlreichen gälischen Glossen, das in Würzburg aufbewahrt wird. Weitere Manuskripte sind in Bamberg, St. Gallen und Schaffhausen zu finden.

Den Missionaren der frühen Zeit folgten vom 9. bis 11. Jahrhundert Ströme irischer Pilger (Scoti vagantes). Die 'peregrinatio' mit dem Heiligen Land oder Rom als Ziel wurde Mode und erfaßte auch Laien. Noch im 11. Jahrhundert sind irische Könige und Adlige als Pilger über Deutschland nach Rom gezogen. Colman, ein Sohn des irischen Hochkönigs Malachias, ist 1092 bei Wien auf unbekannte Weise umgekommen; seine Grabstätte ist im Kloster Melk an der Donau zu finden.

Nachdem ab 795 die irische Insel immer wieder von heidnischen Norsemännern, d.h. Skandinaviern oder Wikingern, heimgesucht wurde, nahm die Zahl der Pilger eher zu. Einige beschlossen, in deutschen Landen zu bleiben. Zu diesen gehörte der Ire Martinus, der 976 eines der Kölner Klöster gründete. Im Jahre 1004 finden wir einen weiteren Iren als Abt dieses Kölner Klosters, den Heiligen Ailél. Auch das dortige St. Pantaleonskloster wurde ab 1042 von einem Landsmann geleitet.

Zuvor schon fühlte sich eine andere Gruppe von Iren, nämlich die Gelehrten, vom Kontinent und der blühenden Kultur der karolingischen Palastschulen angezogen. Diese Iren trugen meist den Beinamen 'Scotus', wie beispielsweise Clemens Scotus, der um 830 am Hofe Lothars lebte und ein bedeutendes mittelalterliches Werk, die *Ars Grammatica*, schrieb.

Besonders hervorzuheben sind Dicuil, Sedulius Scotus und Johannes Scotus Eriugena. Der Letztere entwickelte einen interessanten christlichen Pantheismus, der Gott mit der Natur gleichsetzte.

Marianus Scotus (1028-1082) wurde einer der wichtigsten mittelalterlichen Historiker. Als Mönch in St. Martin in Köln verfaßte er eine umfassende Weltchronik. Von Köln ging er über Paderborn nach Fulda, um 1059 in Würzburg zum Priester geweiht zu werden. Schließlich nahm er seinen Auf-enthalt in Mainz als sogenannter 'inclusus' am Dom. Hier starb er 1082.

Ein zweiter Gelehrter, der sich ebenfalls Marianus Scotus nannte, kam 1067 mit zwei irischen Gefährten, Johannes und Candidus, auf den Michaelsberg bei Bamberg, von dort zog er aber weiter nach Regensburg und ließ sich ebenfalls als 'inclusus' nieder, bis er 1075 die Leitung des

Schottenklosters St. Jakob übernahm. Er starb im Jahre 1083 oder 1086.

ભ

In umgekehrter Richtung wissen wir nur von einem einzigen deutschen Beitrag auf irischem Boden. Zwischen 1127 und 1134 ließ Cormac MacCarthy of Desmond, König von Munster, eine romanische Kirche - Cormac's Chapel - auf dem Felsen von Cashel (dem Sitz der irischen Hochkönige) bauen. Dabei zog er zwei Spezialisten aus Regensburg hinzu, einen Zimmermann namens Conrad und einen Schreiner namens Wilhelm. Sie waren ihm vom irischen Abt Dirmicius aus Regensburg geschickt worden, und zwar zusammen mit einigen Mönchen, die bei Cormac finanzielle Unterstützung für das Regensburger Kloster erbitten sollten. Cormac's Chapel zeigt in der Tat Stilelemente der Regensburger Kirchen aus der romanischen Epoche.

2. Mittelalterliche Episoden

Im hohen und späten Mittelalter sowie zu Beginn der Neuzeit trat nach der anglo-normannischen Invasion Irlands (1169) im deutsch-irischen Verhältnis eine Pause ein. Angesichts der Unterwerfung und des Kampfes der Iren gegen die neuen Herren waren kontinentale Kontakte schwierig. Sofern sie überhaupt stattfanden, lag es (besonders nach der Reformation) nahe, sich eher am benachbarten und katholischen Frankreich zu orientieren, in dem die nach Selbständigkeit strebenden Iren ihre natürlichen Verbündeten hatten. Von dort aus konnten viel leichter Aufstände vorbereitet und, wenn auch meist mit wenig Erfolg, Hilfe bezogen werden als vergleichsweise aus deutschen Landen. Noch wichtiger war, daß in Frankreich katholische Priester ausgebildet werden konnten, was in Irland wegen der *Penal Laws* lange Zeit verboten war.

Ab dem 16. Jahrhundert war das Deutschlandbild der Iren in erster Linie von Luthers Reformation und den zahlreichen Konfessionskonflikten geprägt, für die Iren eine vertraute Szene, da sie selbst ihre eigenen Religionskriege zu erleiden hatten. Im sogenannten Jakobinerkrieg, in dem der katholische Jakob II. dem protestantischen Wilhelm III. (von Oranien) am 12. Juli 1690 in der Schlacht an der Boyne unterlag, kämpften auf protestantischer Seite nicht wenige Söldner aus Hessen und Hannover mit. Der bedeutendste ihrer Anführer war General Friedrich Graf von Schonberg (auch als Schomberg bekannt und 1615 in Heidelberg geboren). Er fiel 1690 an der Boyne und liegt in der Dubliner St. Patricks Kathedrale begraben, wo eine Wandplatte und ein großer Granitstein an ihn erinnert. Interessanterweise scheint er bei seinen deutschen Verwandten so beliebt gewesen zu sein wie bei den irischen Katholiken: die Wandplatte in St. Patricks trägt eine kuriose lateinische

Aufschrift, die der protestantische Dekan (und Schriftsteller) Jonathan Swift (1677-1745) persönlich verfaßt hat.

"Unter diesem Stein liegt der Leichnam von Friedrich, Herzog von Schomberg, der Anno Domino 1690 an der Boyne fiel. Der Dekan und das Domkapitel haben des Herzogs Erben ernsthaft und mehrfach gebeten, ein Denkmal zur Erinnerung an ihren Vater zu errichten. Ohne Ergebnis. Zu guter letzt haben Dekan und Domkapitel diesen Stein aufgestellt, damit wenigstens Du, Fremdling, weißt, wo die leiblichen Überreste Schombergs begraben liegen. Der Ruhm seiner Tapferkeit hatte größere Kraft unter Fremden als die Bande des Blutes unter seinen Anverwandten. Anno Domino 1731."

Üble deutsche Landsknechte hatten auch in Irland einen schlechten Ruf, aber umgekehrt kamen irische Söldner, die in den kontinentalen Heeren des 16. und 17. Jahrhunderts zahlreich zu finden waren, nicht besser davon. Dürer hat 1521 die furchterregenden Gestalten solch irischer Haudegen dargestellt. Während des 30-jährigen Krieges (1618-1648) finden wir prominente irische Namen in Wallensteins Lager: einen Walter Butler, einen Macdonald, einen DeBurgh, einen Geraldine, einen Devereux sowie den Feldkaplan Patrick Taaffe (dessen Nachfahre später Kanzler der österreichischen k.u.k. Monarchie wurde).

Nicht nur von Schiller wissen wir, daß es die irischen Obristen waren, die im Februar 1634 Wallenstein ermordeten. In einer Flugschrift des Jahres 1634 berichtet der Rektor des Jesuitenkollegs in Neuhaus, Caesar de la Couture, von den Ereignissen. Wallenstein war im Begriff, vom kaiserlichen ins gegnerische Lager überzuwechseln und verlangte von seinen irischen Obristen einen Treueid. Diese aber hielten zum Kaiser und beschlossen, den Friedländer kurzerhand zu beseitigen. De la Couture erzählt:

"Da lag die Burg von Eger [...], allwo Leslie sein Logement hielt. Dasselbe hatte er mit fünfzig treuen

irischen Soldaten besetzen lassen. [Dann haben] die Obristen zwei Kapitänen Befehl gegeben, mit zwanzig auserlesenen Iren [...] bewaffnet herbei zu kommen. Devereux stürzte sich auf den Friedländer [...] und hat ihm die Hellebarde durch die Brust gestoßen. Solches ist geschehen den 25. Februarii 1634. "

Auch bei der verheerenden Brandschatzung Heidelbergs durch den französischen Marschall Melac im Jahre 1688 waren viele Iren beteiligt; eine Heidelberger Chronik schildert den Schrecken, den sie verbreiteten. Heidelberger Frauen und Kinder fühlten sich nicht einmal in der Heilig Geist Kirche der Stadt sicher.

Nach ihrer Niederlage im Jahre 1690 waren Tausende von katholischen Anhängern Jakobs II. auf den Kontinent geflohen. Sie sind auch heute noch unter dem Namen 'Wildgänse' bekannt und fanden ihr Auskommen in erster Linie als Söldner und Heeresführer. Unter anderem soll auch der preußische "Soldatenkönig" Friedrich Wilhelm I. sie für seine Garde der "Langen Kerls" sehr geschätzt haben.

CR

Nur einen mittelbar konfessionellen Hintergrund hatte die Ansiedlung von Pfälzern in Irland in den Jahren nach 1709. 13.000 bis 14.000 Deutsche aus der Pfalz machten sich in jenem Jahr auf, um über Rotterdam nach Amerika (Carolina) zu gelangen. Die Motive der Auswanderer waren vielfältig: in erster Linie waren sie aber auf die Verwüstung ihrer Heimat und die ungeheure Not zurückzuführen, die nach den zahlreichen französischen Einfällen in die Pfalz (vor allem im Spanischen Erbfolgekrieg) herrschte. Kurfürst Johann Wilhelm, der nicht in der umkämpften Pfalz, sondern im sicheren Düsseldorf residierte, tat nichts für seine Untertanen. Die mit dem Bruder von Louis XIV. verheiratete Liselotte von der Pfalz schrieb in ihrer berühmten Korrespondenz am 8. Oktober 1695 aus Fontainebleau:

"Mich deucht, der Kurfürst von der Pfalz täte besser, sein Geld an die armen, verderbten Pfälzer anzuwenden, als an Karnevalsvergnügen; das wäre löblicher vor Gott und der Welt."

Ein Bericht aus Holland an den englischen Hof bestätigt diese Betrachtung. Es wird darin erwähnt, die Pfälzer seien geflüchtet *"um die Lasten abzuschütteln, unter der sie ob der Härte des Fürstlichen Regiments und der Abgaben litten, welche sie an den Feind zu leisten hatten."*

Es kamen aber auch Unstimmigkeiten konfessioneller Art mit der Obrigkeit hinzu. Der Treck der Auswanderer geriet in England ins Stocken, da den Organisatoren die Mittel für den Weitertransport nach Amerika ausgingen. Die Not der Pfälzer, die mitten im Winter in London in Zelten lebten, wurde immer größer und entwickelte sich für Königin Anne und die Londoner zu einem politischen Problem. So entstand die Idee, die gestrandeten Deutschen, obwohl der englischen Sprache meist unkundig, unter anderem in Irland anzusiedeln.

Schon zu Zeiten Cromwells ebenso wie nach der Schlacht an der Boyne waren katholische Landbesitzer, die als Rebellen betrachtet wurden, enteignet worden. Etwa 270 Landgüter waren in protestantischen Besitz übergegangen, und nur ein Drittel des Landes (meist unfruchtbarer Boden) verblieb katholischen Bauern. Die protestantischen neuen Herren brauchten Arbeitskräfte, die geeignet und willig waren, ihr Land zu bewirtschaften, aber auch gleichzeitig das protestantische Element im Lande zu stärken. Das englische Parlament debattierte die Lage der Pfälzer und verabschiedete am 23. August 1709 folgende Resolution:

"Daß Ihre Majestät, indem Sie eine Anzahl Protestantischer Pfälzer in dieses Königreich geschickt hat, sehr wohl die Stärkung und Sicherung des Protestantischen Interesses in Irland im Auge gehabt hat. [...] daß dies sehr wohl zur Sicherheit dieses Königreichs beiträgt, daß die genannten Pfälzer ermutigt werden sollten, hier zu siedeln."

Anträge an Königin Anne auf Zuteilung von Pfälzern hatten daraufhin umgehend Erfolg, und 821 Familien wurden nach Irland vermittelt. In Dublin dauerte es allerdings einige Zeit, bis eine entsprechende Kommission sie verteilt hatte, was in erster Linie in der Grafschaft Limerick geschah. Die englische Krone zahlte den Grundherren für die Siedler nicht nur Einstandsgeld, sondern auch noch jahrelang Subsidien.

Die Arbeit im Westen Irlands wurde von den Pfälzern als äußerst mühsam empfunden, zumal viele Handwerker und nicht Bauern waren. 325 Familien gaben im Laufe der Zeit auf, gingen zurück nach England oder gelangten letztlich doch nach Amerika. Die verbliebenen 538 Familien erwiesen sich als fromme, fleißige und friedliche Leute. Zu Spannungen mit der katholischen Bevölkerung kam es kaum. Die Pfälzer heirateten und lebten relativ isoliert unter sich. Der Ethno-graph J.G. Kohl, der 1842 Irland bereiste, berichtete: *"Sie genießen den Ruf der besten Landwirte und der redlichsten Leute. Es sind sehr achtenswerte Menschen."*

Die meisten Pfälzer anglisierten ihre Namen: so wurde beispielsweise aus Schultheiß *Shouldice* oder *Sholdice*, aus Schweizer *Switzer*, aus Meyer *Myer*, aus Scheuer *Schyer*, aus Bubenhauser *Bovenizer* oder aus Imberger *Embury*.

CR

Der Gründer der methodistischen Bewegung, der Engländer John Wesley, der in den Jahren 1750 bis 1789 häufig auf Missionsreisen in Irland war, hatte Anlaß, seiner Frustration über die katholischen Iren Ausdruck zu verleihen. An den frommen Pfälzern hatte er hingegen große Freude, und viele schlossen sich seiner Kirche an.

Irische Pfälzer-Methodisten waren es auch, die für die Methodistenkirche in den USA von erheblicher Bedeutung wurden. Ein Philip Imberger [Embury] (1728 - 1773) wanderte 1760 von Ballingrane in der Grafschaft Limerick nach Amerika aus. Mit Hilfe seiner Glaubensgenossin Barbara Hecks, geb. Ruckle [Röckel], ebenfalls aus Limerick, gründete er die erste amerikanische Methodistengemeinde. Sie umfaßt heute viele Millionen Menschen, von denen so mancher das irische Ballingrane besucht. Die heutigen Nachfahren jener Pfälzer in Irland sind sich ihrer Wurzeln bewußt und pflegen ihre Traditionen in der Irish Palatine Association. In Rathkeale, südlich von Limerick, befindet sich ein Denkmal dieser Anhänglichkeit, das Irische Pfälzer-Museum. Paul Heyse, der 1910 als erster Deutscher den Nobelpreis für Literatur erhielt, hat in jungen Jahren ein Stück über die irischen Pfälzer geschrieben, inspiriert durch Victor Aimé Hubers Erzählung "Die Tochter des Pfälzers" (*Skizzen aus Irland*, 1850). "The Palatine's Daughter" ist im übrigen auch ein bekanntes irisches Volkslied geworden.

Das katholische Irland des 18. Jahrhunderts, sofern es sich überhaupt manifestieren konnte, ging zu Deutschland eher auf Distanz, da es als protestantisch galt. Die protestantische Oberschicht in Irland dachte natürlich anders. Sie zeigte einen gewissen Respekt für die deutsche Kultur. Die Verbundenheit der englischen Krone mit Deutschland spielte sicherlich dabei eine Rolle.

Diese Kreise begrüßten es, daß 1697 deutsche Kaufleute nach dem Jakobinerkrieg in Dublin eine lutherische Gemeinde gründeten. Die Deutschen engagierten Pastor Lichtenstein, der als Miltärpfarrer mit einem Regiment Brandenburger nach Irland gekommen war. 1725 konnte ein Gebetshaus als 'Deutsche Lutherische Kirche der Allerheiligsten Dreieinigkeit' in Dublins Poolbeg Street eingeweiht werden. Heute versteht sich die Lutherische Gemeinde in der St. Finian Kirche in der Adelaide Road Dublins nicht nur als deutsches, sondern auch als irisches Zentrum weltweiten Lutheranertums.

ଔ

Auch im weiteren kulturellen Bereich machte sich eine verstärkte deutsche Präsenz bemerkbar. Händel, damals noch als Deutscher angesehen, ließ 1742 seinen *Messias* in Dublin uraufführen. Auch der bedeutendste Architekt im Irland jener Tage, Richard Castle (abgeleitet von 'Kassel') war Deutscher. Aus einer Kasseler Hugenottenfamilie namens De Ricardi stammend, kam er 1728 nach Dublin.

Viele der großen Häuser und Schlösser im georgianischen Stil, die wir heute in Irland bewundern, wurden von ihm erbaut, z.b. Powerscourt, Russborough, Carton House, Belvedere, aber auch Teile des Trinity College (Printing House, Dining Hall), ebenso wie Leinster House, heute Sitz des irischen Parlaments.

 CR

Recht bemerkenswert ist das Interesse, das die Iren im 18. Jahrhundert während des Siebenjährigen Krieges (1756-63) an Friedrich II., genannt dem Großen, zeigten. Vor allem das Establishment auf der Grünen Insel war von seinen Siegen bei Rossbach und Leuthen (November/Dezember 1757) begeistert. England war in diesem Krieg zunächst Preußens Verbündeter. Das zahlte sich für den Peußenkönig in erster Linie in Subsidien aus. Friedrich war der Held der Zeit, weil er es den wenig geliebten Franzosen 'einmal zeigte', vor allem aber, weil er vermeintlich im Zeichen des Protestantismus über die papistischen Österreicher und Franzosen triumphierte.

Das Mißverständnis konnte kaum größer sein und beruhte auf guter friederizianischer Propaganda. Als Freidenker und Freund Voltaires hatte Friedrich II. mit Religion wenig im Sinn. Doch in Dublin wie in London wurde jedenfalls mehrere Jahre lang Friedrichs Geburtstag gefeiert. Irische Gasthäuser nahmen den Namen 'König von Preußen' an, für eine Weile machte sogar ein Preußen Club in Dublin auf. Eine Straße erhielt den Namen 'Prussia Street', den sie bis zum heutigen Tage noch trägt. Die Begeisterung ebbte allerdings ab, als England nach dem Rücktritt des britischen Premiers William Pitt dem Älteren (1708-88) seine Politik änderte, das Bündnis mit Preußen aufkündigte, und Friedrich der Große für Britannien nicht mehr viel gute Worte zu finden vermochte.

3. Stürmische Zeiten

Mit dem amerikanischen Unabhängigkeitskrieg (1775-1783) und der Französischen Revolution (1789) trat eine Wende in den deutsch-irischen Beziehungen ein. Das allgemeine nationalrevolutionäre Klima schien dem Streben der Iren nach Unabhängigkeit günstig. Die vergeblichen Erhebungen der republikanischen Gesellschaft der 'United Irishmen' unter Wolfe Tone in den Jahren nach 1793 gingen zwar von Frankreich aus. Wolfe Tone hielt sich aber häufig in Hamburg auf, wo seine Schwester verheiratet war, und sie wiederum bot dem Flüchtigen und seiner Frau Obdach. Wolfe Tone war auch in anderen deutschen Städten, 1797 zum Beispiel in Bonn, wo er mit dem dortigen französischen Kommandanten dinierte. Kurioserweise konnte er dabei am anderen, rechten Rheinufer eine Abteilung des O'Donnel'schen Irischen Freicorps (in deren grünen Jacken und roten Hosen) beobachten, Landsleute also, die auf Österreichs Seite gegen die Franzosen kämpften. Im August 1797 war Wolfe Tone in Wetzlar, wo er sich noch einmal bei General Hoche um französische Hilfe bemühte, nachdem dessen Landeunternehmen in der irischen Bantry Bay im Jahre davor gescheitert war.

Hamburg galt auch bei vielen anderen prominenten Aufständischen als Zufluchtsort und idealer Ausgangspunkt, um unentdeckt über England nach Irland zu gelangen. 1796 waren die irischen Rebellen Lord Edward Fitzgerald und Arthur O'Connor dort, um ebenfalls mit den Franzosen Kontakt aufzunehmen. 1798 flüchtete Napper Tandy und eine Reihe anderer Rebellen aus Irland dahin, was sich jedoch als ein tragischer Fehler erwies, da die Stadt Hamburg dem Begehren Englands nachgab, die Iren verhaften und im Oktober 1799 nach London ausliefern ließ.

Das 19. Jahrhundert brachte Irland und Deutschland auf kulturellem Gebiet enger zusammen. Bereits 1775 hatte das Trinity College in Dublin damit begonnen, sich mit der deutschen Sprache und Literatur zu befassen. Die Studenten waren zunächst fast ausschließlich protestantische Theologen. Es wurde zur Tradition, im Anschluß an das Studium Deutschland zu bereisen, um die Stätten Luthers zu besuchen. Erst 1866, mit der Berufung von Albert Maximilian Selss, löste sich der deutsche Lehrstuhl von der theologischen Fakultät. In Galway wurde inzwischen ebenfalls Germanistik betrieben, und zwar von 1849 bis 1869 durch Bensbach, von 1868 bis 1886 durch Geisler, von 1886 bis 1890 durch Steinberger.

Das Interesse der Iren an deutscher Literatur hatte mit der Übersetzung der Werke Klopstocks, Goethes, Schillers sowie anderer deutscher Schriftsteller und Dichter stark zugenommen. Das Verdienst liegt bei den Anhängern der 'Young Ireland' Bewegung, vor allem bei James Clarence Mangan (1803-1849), der als Übersetzer für ihre Veröffentlichung sowohl im Dubliner 'University Magazine' als auch in der *Anthologia Germanica* (22 Teile von 1835 bis 1846) sorgte. Die 'Young Irishmen' um Thomas Davis waren von den Ideen Herders stark beeinflußt. Ihre Zeitschrift 'Nation' druckte Gedichte von Freiligrath, Körner, Rückert und anderen deutschen Romantikern ab. Als Übersetzerin machte sich auch Jane Francesca Elgee, besser bekannt als Oscar Wildes Mutter, einen Namen.

Zur gleichen Zeit sammelten und publizierten auf deutscher Seite die Gebrüder Grimm ihre *Irischen Elfenmärchen,* denen eine weitere Märchensammlung von Killinger, *Erin* genannt, folgte. Beide Bücher wurden in Deutschland recht populär.

Die Romantik, die nicht zuletzt auf die vermeintlich uralte keltische Ossian-Dichtung zurückgeht, welche tatsächlich aber aus der Feder des Schotten James MacPherson und aus den Jahren 1762/63 stammt, ergriff die Intellektuellen Deutschlands und Irlands gleichermaßen.

Wieder stand Herder im Mittelpunkt. Sein Interesse an Linguistik, an der Wiederentdeckung des Mittelalters und damit auch an alten Manuskripten wie z. B. dem Würzburger irischen Glossar, hinterließ bei den Iren einen tiefen Eindruck. Seine Idee von der Nation als der natürlichen Lebenseinheit war es, die zu nationaler Besinnung und zur Beschäftigung mit der keltischen Sprache führte. Nicht nur die Werke der deutschen Romantiker, sondern auch *Werthers Leiden* von Goethe wurden irische Standardlektüre. Ihr Einfluß auf irische Dichter wie z. B. auf Maria Edgeworth wird allgemein anerkannt. Später kam das Interesse an Humboldts preußischer Bildungsreform und an der Philosophie Kants hinzu, besonders nachdem der spätere Provost des Trinity College, John Pentland Mahaffy, 1872 eine Übersetzung von Kants „Kritik der reinen Vernunft" herausgebracht hatte. Er war es auch, der im Trinity College die Beschäftigung mit der deutschen Sprache und Kultur besonders förderte.

Ins Bewußtsein einer breiteren deutschen Öffentlichkeit gelangten die Probleme Irlands erst in der Zeit nach der französischen Revolution. Größere Beachtung der öffentlichen Meinung in der Politik war ein Phänomen der neuen Zeit. Der moderne Journalismus entstand. Die bisher ferne Insel Irland vermochte auch Deutschland näherzurücken. Erstmalig trat jetzt der Kampf der irischen Katholiken um Emanzipation ins Bewußtsein einer europäischen Öffentlichkeit. Oft war jedoch die Diskussion in den Salons der deutschen Bildungsbürger von großer Ignoranz und haarsträubenden Vorurteilen über die Iren geprägt. Von dieser Feststellung kann selbst der große Goethe nicht ausgenommen werden, der in seinen Briefen, Tages- und Jahresheften, in Eckermanns Gesprächen und in *Maxime und Reflexionen* sich als eindeutig anglophil erweist, ungleich seiner Schwiegertochter Ottilie, die zu den ersten begeisterten Irlandfans zu zählen ist, obgleich sie die Insel nie betreten hat. Ihre intime Freundschaft mit dem Iren James Sterling und ihr Gedankenaustausch mit dem Schriftsteller und Journalisten F.G. Kühne beeinflußten sie wohl sehr. Kühne schrieb 1840 den dreibändigen Roman *Rebellen von Irland* und 1856 das Drama *Die Verschwörung von Dublin* und hatte damit beachtlichen schriftstellerischen Erfolg.

Heinrich Heine, der sich auch mit der irischen Frage beschäftigte (ebenfalls ohne die Grünen Insel besucht zu haben), bemühte sich um ein faires Urteil. Obgleich kein Freund der katholischen Kirche, verfolgte Heine den Kampf um die irische Katholikenemanzipation geradezu leidenschaftlich und mit viel Sympathie: 1828, also lange vor der großen Hungersnot, schrieb er in einem Artikel:

"Freilich hätten Europas Völker das heiligste Recht, sich für die Leiden Irlands, mit bewaffneter Hand, zu verwenden, und dieses Recht würde auch ausgeübt werden, wenn nicht das Unrecht stärker wäre."

Es war in jenen Jahren vor allem die katholische Kirche, über die Irland zum Thema wurde. Bereits 1795 war zwischen dem katholischen Priesterseminar in Maynooth und dem deutschen Klerus ein engerer Kontakt entstanden, nachdem der irische kirchliche Faden zu Frankreich wegen der Religionsfeindlichkeit der französischen Revolution fast abgerissen war.

Der Held der Stunde aber war Daniel O'Connell (1775-1847), der 'Befreier', zu dem nicht nur die Iren, sondern auch die deutschen Katholiken aufsahen. Joseph Görres (1776-1848) und die deutsche Katholikenbewegung stand in der ersten Jahrhunderthälfte ganz in seinem Bann. In vielen katholischen Pfarrhäusern und Haushalten Deutschlands soll sein Bild seinerzeit gehangen haben. Selbst der eher unreligiöse Englandfreund Goethe hat ihn erwähnt und einen „mutigen Mann" genannt.

ভ

Der neue Journalismus war nicht das einzige Fenster, das den Blick in fernere Länder öffnete. Bereits am Ende des 18. und verstärkt zu Beginn des 19. Jahrhunderts war es für den deutschen Bildungsbürger möglich, ja fast Mode, Studienreisen in fremde Länder zu machen und anschliessend darüber zu schreiben. Irland war ein neues und beliebtes Ziel. 1791 erschien der erste irische Reiseführer von F.G. Krebel. Vorangegangen waren Reisebeschreibungen von J.J. Volkmann (1784) und dem vielgelesenen K.G. Küttner (1785). Nach Knebels Veröffentlichung folgten irische Reiseberichte von P.A. Nemnich (1807), F. von Raumer (1836), J.G. Kohl (1843), J. Venedey (1844), C. Clement (1845) und M. Hart-mann (1850). Am berühmtesten wurden Fürst Pückler-Muskaus *Irische Tagebücher* von 1826 und 1829. Sie waren, an ihrem Einfluß auf das deutsche Irlandbild gemessen, eine Art Vorläufer des „Irischen Tagebuchs" Heinrich Bölls von 1957. Pücklers Reisebeschreibung war höchst subjektiv und einseitig, da er, eigentlich auf der Suche nach einer mitgiftreichen Braut, vornehmlich in Kreisen protestantischer Notabler und Pastoren verkehrte. Umso beachtlicher ist, daß ihm die ungeheure Not nicht verborgen blieb, in der das einfache Volk lebte, von dem er sagte, *daß "kein Volk poetischer und mit reicherer Phantasie begabt [sei]".* So bemerkte er z.B.,

"daß [...] selbst die [Katholiken-] Emanzipation nicht viel helfen kann; denn das eigentliche Übel besteht darin, daß der meiste Grund und Boden und alle Reichtümer des Landes einem Adel gehören, dessen Hauptinteresse ihn immer zwingen wird, in England zu leben, hauptsächlich aber in der Summe liegt, welche die armen katholischen Irländer jährlich der protestantischen Geistlichkeit opfern müssen. Solange das nicht geändert wird, kann auch kein fester und blühender Zustand der Dinge eintreten."

Friedrich Engels (1820-1895) hatte eine ganz besondere Beziehung zu Irland, nicht zuletzt dank seiner zwei irischen Lebensgefährtinnen, den Schwestern Mary und Lizzy Burns. Sie entstammten der Familie eines irischen Textilfärbers in Manchester, wo Engels (im Exil) die englische Niederlassung des väterlichen Unternehmens leitete. Die zwanzig Jahre dauernde Lebenspartnerschaft mit Mary

Burns endete mit ihrem Tod, und Engels lebte danach für weitere fünfzehn Jahre mit Lizzy Burns zusammen. Die Verbundenheit mit der Familie Burns trug wesentlich dazu bei, daß der 'kapitalistische Unternehmer' Engels sich den Problemen des Proletariats zuwandte. Seine 'irische Familie' war es, die ihn mit den Lebens- und Arbeitsbedingungen der Arbeiter im England jener Jahre vertraut machte. Die Erfahrungen gab Engels an seinen Freund Karl Marx im Londoner Exil weiter, dessen direkter Kontakt mit der proletarischen Wirklichkeit bei weitem nicht so authentisch war.

Dem Einfluß der beiden Irinnen war es auch zu verdanken, daß Engels zeitlebens geradezu leidenschaftlich für die Belange des irischen Volkes Partei ergriff. Von Lizzy, die Engels wenige Stunden vor ihrem Tod 1878 formell ehelichte, erzählt der Schwiegersohn von Karl Marx, der französische Arzt Paul Lafargue, sie sei in "fortgesetzter Verbindung mit Irländern" (Feniern) gestanden und stets über "ihre Komplotte" informiert gewesen. Sicher sei, daß mehr als ein Fenier im Hause Engels Unterschlupf gefunden habe.

Im Mai 1856 reiste Engels mit Mary Burns zum ersten Mal durch Irland. Über die entsetzlichen Zustände nach der Hungersnot berichtete er ausführlich an Karl Marx in London. Mit Lizzy Burns und der Marx Tochter Eleonor ("Tussy") unternahm er im September 1869 eine zweite Irlandreise. Er fand, die Dinge hätten sich nicht wesentlich verändert. Engels war von beiden Reisen so beeindruckt, daß er im Sommer 1870 sich ernsthaft daran setzte, eine umfangreiche Darstellung der Geschichte Irlands zu schreiben, die jedoch ein Fragment blieb. Engels besuchte Irland ein letztes Mal im September 1891, zusammen mit der Burns Nichte Mary Ellen (die zeitweise bei Engels aufwuchs) und mit Louise Kautsky, der geschiedenen Ehefrau von Karl Kautsky, dem ebenfalls im Londoner Exil lebenden deutschen Sozialistenführer. Louise war bis zu Engels Tod 1895 als seine Haushälterin und Privatsekretärin tätig. Mary Ellen Burns, Louise Kautsky und die Marx Kinder waren es auch, die im August 1895 den letzten Willen Engels erfüllten, indem sie die Urne mit seiner Asche in der Irischen See versenkten.

Der bayerische König Ludwig I., der in der Münchner Architekturgeschichte starke Spuren hinterließ, wurde nach 1848 international vor allem als Opfer seiner Liaison mit der Tänzerin Lola Montez bekannt. Nur wenige wissen, daß diese *femme fatale* keineswegs Spanierin, sondern Irin war. Der Name "Lola Montez" war ein Alias, nicht nur ein Künstlername, da die Dame zeitlebens darauf bedacht war, ihre wahre Identität, ihre Herkunft und Vergangenheit im Dunkeln zu halten.

In Wirklichkeit wurde Lola Montez 1820 oder 1821 in Limerick geboren und auf den Namen Gilbert getauft. Die Hochzeit ihrer Eltern ist in der westirischen Tageszeitung *Ennis Chronicle* vom 6. Mai 1820 vermerkt. Während ihr Vater Edward Gilbert sich wohl (als Offizier Königin Victorias) in erster Linie als Brite gesehen haben mochte, war ihre Mutter Eliza dagegen eindeutig irischer Abstammung, die Tochter des angesehenen und reichen Parlamentsabgeordneten Charles Silver Oliver MP von Castle Oliver, einem Gutshof in Kilfinane südlich von Limerick.

Die Ehe des jungen Paares Gilbert entsprach wohl wenig dem Geschmack der Olivers, und es verwundert daher nicht, daß Captain Gilbert sich bald zum Dienst in Indien meldete. 1823 ging er mit Frau und Kind in Bengalen (Kalkutta und Dinapore) zu der Familie der Schwiegereltern auf Distanz. Die Cholera raffte jedoch bald Captain Gilbert hinweg, und die Witwe Gilbert heiratete umgehend einen schottischen Major, Patrick Craigie, der es später zum General bringen sollte.

Nachdem Tochter Eliza, auch Betty genannt, schulreif geworden war, schickte man sie zunächst zur Familie des Stiefvaters Craigie im schottischen Montrose und dann in ein englisches Internat für höhere Töchter. Als Eliza sechzehn Jahre alt war, hielt ihre Mutter (im Heimaturlaub aus Indien in England weilend) es für angebracht, die Tochter schnellstens unter die Haube zu bringen. Die junge Dame weigerte sich jedoch, den ausersehenen Bräutigam, einen sechzigjährigen englischen Oberrichter in Kalkutta, zu ehelichen und floh stattdessen kurzentschlossen nach Irland, und zwar mit einem Protegé ihrer Mutter, Captain Thomas James aus dem irischen Wexford (Mitte Dreißig und wie ihr Vater ebenfalls in Indien in Diensten). Die minderjährige Eliza ließ sich am 23. Juli 1837 in Meath von Thomas James' Bruder, einem Pastor, trauen. Die Ehe der Siebzehnjährigen war kein Erfolg und kam in Indien zu einem schnellen Ende. Die inzwischen Zwanzigjährige, bereits in Indien recht skandalumwittert, segelte nach England zurück. Hier überführte Captain James sie 1841 des Ehebruchs (damals strafbar), und Eliza mußte froh sein, daß es gerichtlich nur zu einer "Trennung von Tisch und Bett" und nicht zur Scheidung kam (weshalb aber alle ihre folgenden Ehen ungültig blieben).

Dies alles war der Presse bekannt und ließ der jungen kapriziösen Schönheit im victorianischen England wenig Wahl, was ihr künftiges Leben anging, nur der Weg zum Theater war eine Alternative. Dem Beispiel der Tänzerin Fanny Elßler, der Mätresse des Wiener Staatsmanns Friedrich von Gentz folgend, wählte Eliza die Karriere einer Tänzerin. Ohne offensichtliches Talent, jedoch ausdrucksstark und vor allem bereit, ihrem Publikum mehr als andere zu zeigen, kam sie (gelegentlich einer Reise mit einem ihrer Liebhaber auf die iberische Halbinsel) auf die Idee, sich aufs Spanische zu verlegen.

Ihre ersten Auftritte in London unter ihrem neuen spanischen Namen Lola Montez endeten mit einem Skandal. Verschmähte Verehrer machten ihre Identität als die ehebrüchige Betty James publik, es blieb ihr nur die Flucht auf den Kontinent. Dort versuchte die feurige und temperamentvolle Irin, der alle eine besondere Ausstrahlung nachsagten, ihr Glück in mehreren Hauptstädten. Ihre Liebschaften mit berühmten Männern wie Franz Liszt und hohen Aristokraten wurden überall zum Tagesgespräch. Sie selbst legte es darauf an, durch exzentrisches Benehmen aufzufallen und Skandale zu inszenieren. So waren ihre Aufenthalte in Brüssel, Berlin, Warschau und Dresden jeweils nur von kurzer Dauer.

Nur in Paris schien die 23jährige fast Wurzeln zu fassen; sie wetteiferte in der Pariser Gesellschaft mit George Sand als emanzipierte Frau, verkehrte nicht nur in höheren

Aristokraten sondern auch Künstlerkreisen (Paul Méry, Alexandre Dumas). Beinahe wäre es zu einer festen Verbindung mit dem Redakteur einer einflußreichen Tageszeitung gekommen. Als dieser aber bei einem Duell ihretwegen ums Leben kam, sah Lola Montez sich erneut in einen gerichtlichen Skandal verwickelt und genötigt, das Land zu verlassen.

Nach Zwischenstationen in Bonn und Baden-Baden erschien Lola Anfang Oktober 1846 in München, der Residenz des recht autokratischen Ludwig I. Bekannt war er nicht nur wegen seiner Leidenschaft für Architektur und großangelegte Bauten (München verdankt ihm sein klassizistisches Stadtbild), sondern auch für einen wohlentwickelten Sinn für weibliche Schönheit, der sich unter anderem in der 'Galerie der 36 Schönheiten' im Schloß Nymphenburg manifestiert. Lola, der man zunächst (mangels Ausweispapiere) einen Auftritt in München verwehrt hatte, erwirkte am 7. Oktober 1846 eine Audienz beim König. Eine große königliche Romanze nahm ihren Anfang.

Ludwig verfiel der vermeintlichen spanischen Adligen völlig (sie nannte sich jetzt Maria Dolores von Porris und Montes). Er erfüllte ihr - gegen den Widerstand mehrerer bayerischer Kabinette - so ziemlich alle Wünsche: von einer großzügigen Apanage über das Stadtpalais in der Barerstraße bis hin zum Titel der 'Gräfin von Landsfeld'. All das wäre in damaliger Zeit an sich in königlichen Kreisen kein einmaliger Vorgang gewesen, hätte Lola Montez nicht den Ehrgeiz gehabt, sich in aller Öffentlichkeit in die Staatsgeschäfte und die Personalpolitik ihres königlichen Liebhabers und der bayerischen Regierung einzumischen. Dabei trieb sie vor allem ein tiefer Haß gegen die Jesuiten und deren Einfluß auf das öffentliche Leben in Bayern. Gepaart mit allerhand provozierenden Eigenheiten verschaffte ihr das in kurzer Zeit ein Heer von Feinden.

Ausgelöst durch eine Studentenrevolte wegen der Entlassung von Professoren und der Schließung der Universität kam es zu einem wahren Volksaufstand gegen die Mätresse des Königs. Die Volksmassen zwangen Lola Montez, aus der Stadt zu fliehen. Bald darauf verband sich der Zorn des Volkes mit den allgemeinen 48er Unruhen. Am 19. März 1848 sah sich der König gezwungen abzudanken. Zur erwarteten Vereinigung der beiden Liebenden am Ruhesitz des Monarchen in Nizza kam es nicht. Lola, der Affaire mit einem Studenten während ihrer Münchner königlichen Liaison überführt, verlor die Gunst und Unterstützung Ludwigs. Eliza Gilbert wanderte schließlich nach Australien und in die USA aus, wo sie zunächst als skandalumwitterte Tänzerin, dann als „femme fatale" der europäischen Höfe zu überleben versuchte, indem sie gegen Entgelt aus ihren Memoiren vorlas. Sie starb 41-jährig und völlig verarmt im Jahre 1861 in den Armen eines irischen Pastors in New York. Ludwig dagegen verschied sieben Jahre später in Nizza.

ᘓᖇ

Der Geist Herders und die Romantik der ersten Hälfte des 19. Jahrhunderts waren der Nährboden für einen neuen Wissenszweig: die Keltologie. Sie sollte zum zentralen Punkt der deutsch-irischen Kulturbeziehungen werden. Franz Bopp hatte im Dezember 1838 mit einem Vortrag in Berlin den Start-schuß gegeben, indem er eine wissenschaftliche Befassung mit den keltischen Sprachen initiierte.

Als 1853 die lateinisch geschriebene *Grammatica Celtica* des Gymnasiallehrers Caspar Zeuss aus dem bayerischen Kronach erschien, galt das als eine wahre Sensation. Die Würzburger irischen Glossen hatten ihn zu diesem Lebenswerk veranlaßt. 1864 stellte Kiepert den Zusammenhang zwischen den keltischen und den indogermanischen Sprachen her, und zwischen deutschen und irischen Philologen entstand ein dauerhafter Kontakt. Dazu trug besonders der irische Archäologe John O'Donovan bei, der auf Vorschlag Jakob Grimms 1856 korrespondierendes Mitglied der Königlich Preußischen Akademie geworden war. An dieser Stelle muß auch der deutsche Sanskrit-Forscher Rudolf Thomas Siegfried genannt werden, der - unterstützt von C.F. Lottner - am Dubliner Trinity College lehrte und sich mit keltischen Studien befaßte. Der Engländer Whitley Stokes, der später selbst als Keltologe berühmt werden sollte, war Siegfrieds Schüler und über ihn kam eine enge Zusammenarbeit mit dem berühmten deutschen Keltologen Ernst Windisch zustande. Die abgelegenen Aran Inseln übten auf die deutschen Forscher eine besondere Faszination aus. Der dort gesprochene Dialekt schien hervorragend geeignet, das alte Keltisch zu studieren. Deutsche Wissenschaftler wie Franz Nikolaus Fink, Hermann Osthoff, Heinrich Zimmer und Kuno Meyer waren deshalb mehrfach Gäste der Inselbewohner. Kuno Meyer schrieb Whitley Stokes beispielsweise einen Feriengruß von den Arans:

"Lieber Dr. Stokes, wir sind hier sehr glücklich [...] Der Pfarrer, Vater O'Donohue, ist äußerst freundlich zu uns. Ich schreibe so viele Wörter, Sätze etc., wie ich irgendwie aufschnappen kann, auf. Sie verwenden hier offensichtlich viel weniger englische Lehnworte als auf der Insel Achill."

1892 veröffentlichte Fink in Marburg ein Werk über den Aran Dialekt, nachdem Windisch schon 1880 seine Geschichte der keltischen Philologie und Alfred Holder 1891 sein alt-keltisches Wörterbuch herausgebracht hatten. Inzwischen waren auch in Deutschland die „Zeitschrift für keltische Philologie" und das „Archiv für keltische Lexikographie" gegründet worden.

Die deutsch-irische keltologische Fachwelt bildete schon lange eine enge Gemeinschaft. Ins Bewußtsein einer breiteren irischen Öffentlichkeit aber trat die Wiederentdeckung der irischen Sprache und der deutsche Beitrag dazu erst zu Beginn des 20. Jahrhunderts, vornehmlich durch die Arbeiten Zimmers, Thurneysens, Pokornys, besonders aber durch die Verdienste Kuno Meyers. Der Faden zwischen den deutschen und irischen Keltologen riß selbst in schwer-sten Zeiten nicht ab. Als 1922 Thurneysen seine *Keltische Grammatik* in Deutschland veröffentlichen wollte, konnte er das nur mit finanzieller Unterstützung der jungen irischen Regierung tun, da die Deutschen keine öffentlichen Mittel dafür hatten.

In der zweiten Hälfte des 19. Jahrhunderts nahmen endlich auch die kommerziellen Beziehungen zwischen Deutschland und Irland an Intensität zu. Der Deutsche Bund (1815-1866) und das Kaiserreich (1871-1918) unterhielten in fast allen größeren irischen Hafenstädten (Dublin, Belfast, Cork, Limerick, Derry, Waterford, Dundalk) Wahl- oder Honorarkonsulate, und der bilaterale Handel begann zu blühen. Dazu trug der etwas späte, aber darum um so schnellere industrielle Aufschwung Deutschlands im 19. Jahrhundert bei. Dies wiederum zog unternehmerische Iren an. Am erfolgreichsten und berühmtesten wurde der Dubliner William Thomas Mulvany (1806-1885). Er war der Sohn eines bekannten Kunstmalers, dessen Bilder noch heute in der Dubliner National Gallery zu sehen sind. Als Tiefbau-Ingenieur und Angestellter des Schiffahrtsamtes (Board of Works) war er zunächst maßgeblich am Ausbau des Kanalsystems in Irland beteiligt. Mit 43 Jahren verließ er 1849 die Grüne Insel und ging nach Deutschland. An der Ruhr gründete er Kohlebergwerke (Untertagebergbau), die sich bald als höchst ertragreich erwiesen. Mulvany gab ihnen die Namen Shamrock (1856 in Gelsenkirchen) und Hibernia (1857 in Herne). Später kam noch die Zechengesellschaft Erin hinzu, die aber schon 1882 vom preußischen Staat übernommen wurde. Die Hibernia ging erst in den 70er Jahren dieses Jahrhunderts in der Ruhrkohle AG der Veba auf. Ein Eisenwerk in Duisburg, der Kanal zwischen Rhein-Weser-Elbe, der Mittellandkanal, der Dortmund-Ems-Kanal gehen ebenfalls auf Mulvanys Initiative zurück. Er gilt ferner als Gründer der Düsseldorfer Börse, wo eine Büste ebenso an ihn erinnert wie in der Veba-Hauptverwaltung. Mulvany starb 1886 als schwerreicher und hoch geehrter Mann und liegt in Düsseldorf begraben.

CR

Inzwischen hatten die Deutschen die Revolution von 1848 erlebt, und Bismarck hatte das Kaiserreich geschaffen. Die

Deutschen hatten also viel mit sich selbst zu tun. Dennoch verfolgten vor allem die deutschen Katholiken seit der Großen Hungersnot (1846-49) die irische Frage mit wachsendem Verständnis und Mitgefühl, was sich jedoch in der Politik des Reiches nicht niederschlug. Auf der rein politischen Ebene blieb das deutsche Verhältnis zu Irland ein Element der Beziehungen zu Großbritannien. Andererseits sahen die Iren Deutschland durch ihre konfessionelle Brille, was das irische Deutschlandbild entscheidend prägte. Der deutsch-französische Krieg 1870/71 wurde so in Irland weniger als ein Kampf um die nationale Einheit Deutschlands als ein Konflikt zwischen der katholischen keltischen Brudernation Frankreich und dem protestantischen Preußen gesehen. Die Iren demonstrierten ihre Gefühle unter anderem dadurch, daß sie einen Sanitätszug nach Frankreich entsandten, und daß sie beispielsweise protestierten, als der deutsche Honorarkonsul in Limerick, J.Spraight [Specht - ein irischer Pfälzer], es im August und September 1871 wagte, die preußische Flagge zu hissen. Pro-preußische Manifestationen gab es bezeichnenderweise 1871 nur in eher protestantischen nordirischen Städten wie Enniskillen und Ballymena.

Was die Iren nach der Reichsgründung 1871 in erster Linie an Deutschland interessierte, war der Kulturkampf, d.h. die Auseinandersetzung Bismarcks mit dem deutschen Katholizismus. Als schließlich die deutschen Katholiken sich mit ihrem Widerstand durchsetzten und Bismarck sich nach 1878 mit der Kirche und Papst Leo XIII. arrangierte, hinterließ dies bei den katholischen Iren einen starken Eindruck. Das irische Bild vom protestantischen Deutschland erfuhr eine wesentliche Revision, zumal man irischerseits über den zunehmenden Trend zur Säkularisierung des Lebens im liberalen Frankreich entsetzt war.

Die irische Bildkorrektur traf zusammen mit dem Zeitgeist, der nach 1871 immer nationalistischere Züge annahm; das wirtschaftlich und politisch aufstrebende und erfolgreiche Zweite Deutsche Reich rückte immer mehr in den Interessenkreis der irischen Nationalisten, ob sie nun um 'Home Rule' rangen oder auf radikale Trennung von Groß-britannien drängten. Man sah in Deutschland viele Parallelen und Vorbilder, da dieses Deutschland binnen kurzer Zeit aus einem Agrar- zu einem Industriestaat und darüber hinaus zum großen Herausforderer britischen Hegemonialstrebens in Europa geworden war. Es ist nicht verwunderlich, daß beispielsweise Arthur Griffith sich in der Unabhängigkeitsbewegung Cumann na nGaedheal und in ihrer Nachfolgeorganisation Sinn Féin intensiv mit dem Modell Deutschland, vor allem mit den Wirtschaftstheorien Friedrich Lists befaßte, oder daß im Oktober 1899 ein hochpolitischer deutsch-irischer Gleichklang dadurch entstehen konnte, daß die irischen Republikaner unter Führung von John MacBride (1916 nach dem Osteraufstand hingerichtet) eine Irische Brigade nach Südafrika entsandten, um - wie das Reich - auf der Seite der Buren zu stehen.

ଓଃ

Doch der politische Spielraum blieb eng: der Hauptakzent deutsch-irischer Beziehungen lag am Ende des 19. und zu Beginn des 20. Jahrhunderts weiterhin im Bereich der Kultur.

1884 hatte Michael Cusack, sehr von der deutschen Turnerbewegung Jahns beeinflußt, die Gaelic Athletic Association (GAA) gegründet. 1883 wurde die Conradh na Gaeilge, die Gälische Liga, ins Leben gerufen. Ihr erster Vorsitzender war bis 1913 Douglas Hyde (1860-1949), der später von 1938 bis 1945 Staatspräsident werden sollte. Hyde war seit 1893 mit Lucy Kurtz verheiratet. Sie entstammte einer deutschen Familie aus Württemberg, die zuerst nach Odessa, dann 1815 nach England emigriert war. In dieser Zeit spielte auch die National Literary Society um W. B. Yeats und T.W. Rolleston eine Rolle, die sich intensiv mit der deutschen Literatur beschäftigte. In den USA wurde der Gedanke ver-folgt, Iro-Amerikaner und Deutsch-Amerikaner zur Vertretung gemeinsamer Interessen einander näher zu bringen. Dieser Plan sollte bis in den 1.Weltkrieg hinein eine Rolle spielen.

ଓଃ

Prominenteste Persönlichkeit im deutsch-irischen Verhältnis war jedoch Kuno Meyer. Als 1898 die Schulkommission in Dublin plante, die irische Sprache erneut aus dem Schulplan zu streichen, appellierte Douglas Hyde an die bekanntesten Keltologen Europas. Die Reaktion und die Vorschläge Kuno Meyers, der seit 1884 Dozent für Deutsch in Liverpool war, gefielen Hyde besonders. 1901 nahmen Kuno Meyer und Zimmer am pan-keltischen Kongress in Dublin teil. Douglas Hyde war von Kuno Meyer so beeindruckt, daß er ihn 1903 zum ersten Direktor der School of Irish Learning in Dublin berief. In seiner Rede vor den Kongressteilnehmern hatte Kuno Meyer unter anderem gesagt:

"Ich kenne keinen Iren oder keine Irin, die nicht im Innersten ihres Herzens auf das schöne Vaterland sehr stolz ist und es liebt aus einer vielschichtigen Vergangenheit heraus. [...] Aus dieser Liebe wird einmal ein weiteres und größeres Irland entspringen als die Insel voll Parteilichkeit und Spaltung jetzt."

Meyer arbeitete von diesem Zeitpunkt an auch in der Gälischen Liga aktiv mit und wurde so bekannt, daß ihm im April 1912 die Ehrenbürgerschaft der Stadt Dublin und im September desselben Jahres die der Stadt Cork verliehen wurde. Im 1.Weltkrieg war Kuno Meyer als "Feind" im (britischen) Irland nicht mehr erwünscht, und beide Ehren wurden ihm demzufolge aberkannt. Sie wurden ihm nach der Unabhängigkeit - wenn auch posthum - im Jahre 1920 wieder neu verliehen.

Kuno Meyer verstand die Keltologie als eine Wissenschaft, die auch einen kulturpolitisch-völkischen Auftrag haben sollte. Es verwundert daher nicht, daß er - 1911 auf den Lehrstuhl Zimmers in Berlin berufen - mit den 'Alldeutschen' in engster Verbindung stand. Gleichzeitig war Kuno Meyer (ebenso wie Schwester Toni und Bruder Eduard Meyer) mit Sir Roger Casement befreundet, der ihm auch wertvolle Kontakte in den USA vermittelte. In der Tat ging Kuno Meyer im November 1914 in die USA, um unter anderem - mit der Reichsregierung abgestimmt - die irisch-amerikanischen Kreise auf 'deutschem Kurs' zu halten und eine Allianz zwischen Großbritannien und den USA gegen Deutschland zu verhindern. Tatsächlich kam es zunächst zwischen den irisch- und den deutsch-amerikanischen Vereinigungen zu Absprachen und zur Zusammenarbeit. Diese endete jedoch mit dem Eintritt der USA in den 1. Weltkrieg, ein Ereignis, das Kuno Meyer im Mai 1917 nach Berlin zurückkehren ließ. Hier setzte er sich auf Vortragsreisen weiterhin unermüdlich für die nationalistischen irischen Ziele ein.

Die Beziehungen zwischen Deutschland und Irland wurden bis zum 1.Weltkrieg nicht nur von Keltologen wie Kuno Meyer, sondern auch von anderen Persönlichkeiten getragen. In dieser Zeit stießen zu der deutschen Kolonie, die traditionell aus Handwerkern (Uhrmachern, Juwelieren, Schneidern, Metzgern, Köchen) oder aus Lehrern und Gouvernanten bestand, zum ersten Mal auch Künstler, vor allem Musiker. Als erster kam 1888 Heinrich Bewerunge (1862-1923) aus Westfalen, um am College von Maynooth Kirchenmusik zu lehren. In Cork entstand zunächst mit Theo Gmür und Conrad Swartz, dann mit Aloys Fleischmann eine wahre Tradition deutscher Organisten und Musiker. Fleischmann gründete die dortige, sehr beliebte Musikschule. Sein Sohn führte das Erbe bis zu seinem Tod 1995 weiter. Von 1887 bis 1891 lehrte der deutsche Dominikaner Thomas Esser in Maynooth Philosophie. Die Bande zwischen den katholischen Kirchen in beiden Ländern wurden immer enger. Pilgerreisen nach Maria Laach, Würzburg, Regensburg und Oberammergau wurden geradezu Mode.

4. Der Große Krieg - Die Casement Story

Erst nach 1912 kam eine rein politische Komponente in die deutsch-irischen Beziehungen. In ihrem Mittelpunkt steht Sir Roger Casement; als anglo-irischer Protestant 1864 in der Grafschaft Antrim geboren, war er Konsularbeamter in britischen Diensten gewesen und im Juli 1912 nach Irland zurückgekehrt, um sich ganz in den Dienst der republikanisch-nationalistischen irischen Unabhängigkeitsbewegung zu stellen. Die deutsch-britischen Beziehungen waren wegen der Flotten- und Kolonialpolitik des Reiches sehr angespannt. Casement nahm ganz den deutschen Standpunkt ein und war bemüht, sich zunächst um die deutsch-irischen Wirtschaftsbeziehungen zu kümmern. Wie Arthur Griffith griff er die Ideen Friedrich Lists auf und wäre beinahe mit dem Projekt einer Umleitung des deutschen Hamburg-Amerika-Verkehrs über den irischen Hafen Cobh (anstelle des britischen Southampton) erfolgreich gewesen. Der 1.Weltkrieg kam jedoch dazwischen.

Im November 1913 spitzte sich der englisch-irische Gegensatz so zu, daß es zur Aufstellung illegaler irischer Freiwilligenverbände, der 'Irish Volunteers' und der 'Ulster Volunteers', kam. Die Hauptschwierigkeit beider entgegengesetzter Gruppen war es, Waffen zu bekommen. Der Blick richtete sich nach Deutschland: nicht nur die katholischen Nationalisten, sondern auch die protestantischen Unionisten in Ulster, die ebenfalls - wenn auch aus anderen, entgegengesetzten Gründen - mit London im Konflikt waren, suchten ihr Waffenproblem in Deutschland zu lösen. Hintergrund war das Ringen um "Home Rule" für ganz Irland. Die Unionistenführer Edward Carson und James Craig lehnten sie radikal ab; der Slogan hieß: 'Home Rule is Rome Rule'. Schon 1911 war Carson so weit gegangen, im Unterhaus lautstark zu erklären, er ziehe Kaiser Wilhelm II. dem Führer der irischen Nationalisten, John Redmond MP (dem potentiellen irischen Ministerpräsidenten im Falle der Home Rule), vor. Man spielte in den Kreisen Carsons und Craigs sogar mit der Idee, die protestantischen Mächte Europas zu Hilfe zu rufen.

Carson, häufiger Kurgast in Baden-Baden und Bad Homburg, traf sich in der Tat 1913 dort mit Kaiser Wilhelm II.; dabei soll Carson Wilhelm II. erklärt haben, er (der Kaiser) habe in Nordirland viele Freunde, falls es zu einem Krieg mit England komme. Beide Parteien kauften insgeheim Waffen in Deutschland; im nordirischen Larne wurden Anfang 1914 für die unionistischen Ulster Volunteers 35.000 deutsche Mausergewehre und 2½ Millionen Schuß Munition angelandet. Im Juli desselben Jahres waren die Nationalisten an der Reihe, wenn auch aus finanziellen Gründen in bescheidenerem Umfang. In Howth bei Dublin wurden aus Deutschland 900 Gewehre und 25.000 Schuß Munition an Land gebracht. Maßgeblich beteiligt waren Darrell Figgis und Robert Erskine Childers, dessen Yacht *Asgard* zu diesem Einsatz verwendet wurde. Bezeichnend war, daß die englischen Sicherheitskräfte versuchten, der Ladung von Howth habhaft zu werden, während sie in Larne den Schmuggel durchgehen ließen.

ය

Unmittelbar nach dem Ausbruch des 1.Weltkriegs erklärte der Führer der irischen (parlamentarischen) Nationalisten, John Redmond, seine Partei werde die britische Regierung im Krieg voll unterstützen. Er strebte an, die Verteidigung der Grünen Insel den 'Irish' und den 'Ulster Volunteers' gemeinsam zu überlassen und so die britische Armee zu "entlasten". Die Offerte wurde in London, das beiden Seiten mißtraute, abgelehnt und hatte eine negative Folge: die Politik Redmonds führte zu einer Spaltung des nationalistischen Lagers. Die große Mehrheit stand hinter Redmond, aber eine militante Minderheit war entschlossen, Großbritannien im Krieg auf keinen Fall zu unterstützen, sondern Kontakt mit dem Deutschen Reich zu suchen und den Krieg für einen bewaffneten Aufstand der Iren zu nutzen;

die Devise hieß: "Englands Gefahr ist Irlands Chance". Zu diesem Lager gehörten Patrick Pearse, Joseph Plunkett, Thomas MacDonagh, Eoin MacNeil und andere prominente Mitglieder der Irish Republican Brotherhood (IRB) und Sinn Féin (SF), vor allem aber Sir Roger Casement. Die allgemeine britische Wehrpflicht erstreckte sich zwar nicht auf Irland, London mußte um irische Freiwillige werben. Aufgrund der wirtschaftlichen Lage der meisten katholischen Iren war das nicht allzu schwer. Insgesamt 90.000 bis 100.000 Iren haben zwischen August 1914 und April 1916 auf britischer Seite gekämpft; von den etwa 178.000 'National Volunteers' sollen sich jedoch nur 10.000 gemeldet haben.

Das darf nicht darüber hinwegtäuschen, daß die Stimmung der breiten Masse der irischen Bevölkerung während des 1.Weltkriegs, so wenig pro-britisch sie gewesen sein mag, keineswegs eindeutig pro-deutsch war. Nur die relativ kleine radikal-republikanische Minderheit, die Roger Casement mit anderen zusammen vertrat, setzte ganz auf Deutschland. Wichtig war, daß Redmonds Politik die Iro-Amerikaner enttäuschte. Ihre Anführer, John Devoy und McGarrity, machten den Weg für massive finanzielle Unterstützung des pro-deutschen republikanischen Flügels frei. Casement war zu diesem Zweck mehrfach in den USA. Mit Hilfe der dortigen deutschen Botschaft stand er mit beiden in engem Kontakt. Der Leiter der Botschaft war Graf Bernstorff, ihr Verbindungsmann der stark nationalistisch engagierte Militärattaché von Papen (1932 Reichskanzler und 1933 Hitlers Steigbügelhalter). Es ging nicht nur um Geld und Waffen. Casement und Devoy verfaßten im Rahmen dieser Kontakte unter anderem auch eine Petition an Kaiser Wilhelm II., die in der Bitte gipfelte, die Befreiung Irlands zum Kriegsziel der Mittelmächte zu erklären (was nicht geschah).

Mit der Finanzhilfe irisch-amerikanischer Kreise im Hintergrund begab sich Casement nach Deutschland und traf dort am 1. November 1914 ein. In Berlin war er mittlerweile längst eingeführt. Bereits am 12. November 1914 erwirkte er eine Abmachung mit dem Unterstaatssekretär im Auswärtigen Amt, Arthur Zimmermann. Mit dieser sagte die Reichsregierung einer künftigen irischen Regierung ihre volle moraische Unterstützung bei der Errichtung eines unabhängigen Staates zu. Diese Absichtserklärung wurde am 28. Dezember 1914 durch den Beschluß ergänzt, aus den Reihen britischer Kriegsgefangener die katholischen Iren auszusondern und mit ihnen eine Irische Brigade für den Einsatz in einem irischen Unabhängigkeitskrieg zu bilden. Die Klausel wurde übrigens dahingehend erweitert, daß der Einsatz auch in anderen Unabhängigkeitskämpfen in Frage käme, wie zum Beispiel in Ägypten. Eine derartige Vereinbarung war mit den Freunden in Dublin keineswegs abgesprochen, und somit ein klarer Alleingang Casements. Die Irische Brigade war ein Mißerfolg ersten Ranges: lediglich 55 Kriegsgefangene irischer Abstammung meldeten sich, obgleich Casement die Gefangenenlager persönlich besuchte. Er hatte bereits zwei irische Dominikaner aus Rom, Pater Crotty und Pater O'Gorman, zur Truppenbetreuung kommen lassen. Casement erreichte jedoch eine Sonderbehandlung für alle irischen Gefangenen, unabhängig davon, ob sie sich zur Brigade gemeldet hatten oder nicht. Das Häuflein der Freiwilligen in der Irischen Brigade wurde später nach Danzig verlegt und löste sich dort im Laufe des Krieges mehr oder weniger wieder auf. Von der ganzen Episode blieb nur eines: die Uniform dieser Brigade diente als Vorbild für die erste Uniform der Irischen Armee.

Casement war ziemlich frustriert und konzentrierte sich infolgedessen auf die Waffenfrage. Im April 1915 traf mit Joseph Plunkett in Berlin Verstärkung ein. Er besprach mit Casement den in Dublin geplanten bewaffneten Aufstand. Zusammen mit Devoy in den USA bemühten sie sich, die deutsche Waffenlieferung für diese Erhebung zu koordinieren. Zu ihrer Enttäuschung lehnten die Deutschen es ab, militärisches Personal zur Verfügung zu stellen. Devoy einigte sich aber über die deutsche Botschaft in Washington auf eine größere Waffenlieferung. Über deren Umfang gab es Mißverständnisse: Casement ging von 200.000 Gewehren und Maschinengewehren aus, in Wirklichkeit verließ aber nur die mit Devoy vereinbarte Menge, nämlich 20.000 Gewehre und 100.000 Maschinengewehre (nebst Munition) auf dem als norwegischen Frachter *Aud* getarnten *MS Libau* Wilhelmshaven. Casement fühlte sich hintergangen.

Die *Libau/Aud* erreichte die Bucht von Tralee am Gründonnerstag 1916. Sie war nicht mit Funk ausgestattet und konnte daher unterwegs weder aus Berlin noch aus Washington erfahren, daß der Termin der Entladung kurzfristig auf Ostersonntag verschoben worden war. Nach einem Tag gefährlichen Wartens wurde die *Libau/Aud* dann auch prompt von britischen Kriegsschiffen aufgebracht und in den Kriegshafen Cobh geschleppt. Hier hatte Kapitän Karl Spindler allerdings noch die erstaunliche Geistesgegenwart, das Schiff samt Ladung vor den Augen der Briten zu versenken.

Von alledem in Unkenntnis, befand sich Casement auf dem deutschen U-Boot *U19*, das ihn - koordiniert mit der Entladung der *Libau/Aud* - an Land setzen sollte. Mit ihm waren noch Robert Monteith, ein des Landes verwiesener Instrukteur der 'National Volunteers' und ein Mann namens Bailey, der sich zu der deutschen Irischen Brigade gemeldet hatte. Beteiligt an dieser U-Boot-Operation war auch ein junger Marineoffizier namens Ernst Heinrich von Weizsäcker, später Staatssekretär im Auswärtigen Amt Hitlers und Vater des Bundespräsidenten Richard Karl von Weizsäcker (geb. 1920).

Casement wurde am Karfreitag 1916 bei Tralee am Banna Strand an Land gesetzt. Dieser Ort scheint aus heutiger Sicht wegen seiner breiten Einsehbarkeit für das Vorhaben höchst ungeeignet. Es verwundert nicht, daß Casement und seine Mannen in kürzester Zeit entdeckt und verhaftet werden konnten. Man brachte ihn nach London, wo er wegen Landesverrat zum Tod durch den Strang verurteilt und am 3. August 1916 hingerichtet wurde. Erst 1965 war es möglich, ihn mit einem Staatsakt auf dem Dubliner Friedhof von Glasnevin beizusetzen.

CR

Der Osteraufstand 1916, vom Dubliner Hauptpostamt ausgehend, fand ohne Casement und ohne deutsche Waffen statt. So heldenhaft er auch erscheinen mag, endete er wie die Bemühungen Casement mit einem dramatischen Zusammenbruch. Nur wenige der beteiligten Führer der Bewegung (darunter wegen seiner amerikanischen Staatsangehörigkeit Eamon de Valera) überlebten. Die brutale britische Reaktion trieb jedoch dem radikalen irischen Flügel weite Kreise in Irland und auch in den USA zu. Obgleich der deutsche Beitrag mit der *Libau/Aud* und Casement ein Ende gefunden hatte, blieb der Verdacht der Briten bestehen, die IRB und Sinn Féin arbeiteten weiterhin eng mit Berlin zusammen. Tatsächlich hatte sich Sinn Féin aufgrund der Ereignisse für die restliche Zeit des Krieges zu einem mehr oder minder neutralen Verhalten durchgerungen.

Als aber im April 1918 Joseph Dowling, ein weiteres ehemaliges Mitglied der deutschen Irischen Brigade auf Crabbe Island vor der irischen Küste von einem deutschen U-Boot abgesetzt wurde und mit Sinn Féin Kontakt aufnahm, verhafteten die Briten nicht nur Dowling, sondern auch fast die gesamte Sinn Féin Führung (über siebzig Personen) und zwar unter dem Vorwand einer "deutschen Verschwörung". Unter anderem wurden de Valera, Griffith und Countess Markievicz inhaftiert.

Zu einem letzten deutsch-irischen Kriegskontakt kam es im Oktober 1917 in der Schweiz. Der spätere Bürgermeister von Cork, Terence MacSwiney, dessen Frau mit dem deutschen Gesandten in Bern, Romberg, verschwägert war, versuchte noch einmal, mit der Reichsregierung Verbindung aufzunehmen. Seit dem Casement Fiasko war Berlin jedoch vorsichtig geworden; man hatte aber auch Ende 1917 schon andere Sorgen.

Wie weit allerdings die Überlegungen irischer Nationalisten gingen, zeigen die ernsthaften Erwägungen von wenigstens drei der Teilnehmer am Osteraufstand - Thomas Clarke, Joseph Plunkett, Patrick Pearse - im Falle der Unabhängigkeit Irlands die alte monarchische Verfassung von 1782 wieder in Kraft zu setzen und einen deutschen Prinzen als Staatsoberhaupt vorzuschlagen; bestimmend war die Über-legung, daß im Fall eines deutschen Sieges eine enge Anlehnung an das Deutsche Reich notwendig sein würde. Man dachte an den sechsten und jüngsten Sohn Wilhelm II.,

Prinz Joachim (1890-1920). Dieses Kuriosum zeigt im übrigen, wie der Begriff 'republikanisch' gedeutet wurde: synonym mit nationaler Emanzipation und nicht notwendigerweise mit Ablehnung einer monarchischen Staatsform.

છ

Das Kapitel "Deutschland und Irland im 1.Weltkrieg" schloß mit einem besonders tragischen Ereignis: wenige Wochen vor der deutschen Novemberrevolution versenkte ein deutsches U-Boot am 11. Oktober 1918 die *RMS Leinster* der City of Dublin Steampacket Company. Das Torpedo traf das Schiff auf dem Weg nach Holyhead (Wales), etwa eine Stunde vor dem Dubliner Vorort Dun Laoghaire. Von 771 Passagieren an Bord (darunter 482 Soldaten) ertranken 501. Es war die letzte Aktion dieser Art im 1.Weltkrieg. Es ist nicht geklärt, ob durch dieses schreckliche Ereignis die Waffen-stillstandsverhandlungen des Reichskanzlers Prinz Max von Baden (am 4. Oktober begonnen und am 11. November 1918 abgeschlossen) verzögert wurden, und ob dadurch weitere unnötige Opfer des sinnlosen Krieges entstanden sind.

5. Weimar

Nach dem 1.Weltkrieg war die Lage sowohl in Deutschland als auch in Irland völlig verändert. Es begann ein neues Kapitel deutsch-irischer Beziehungen. Ein kurzer Blick auf die Lage der beiden 'underdogs' jener Jahre - Irland und Deutschland - scheint angezeigt.

In Berlin herrschte zunächst Revolution, Scheidemann rief die Republik aus. Die Weimarer Verfassung wurde angenommen und eine Reichsregierung nach der anderen begann ihren Hürdenlauf.

In Dublin gründeten 30 der 73 irischen Unterhaus-abgeordneten (36 davon im Gefängnis) ein irisches Parlament, den Dáil Éireann. Die Atmosphäre war geprägt von irischer Euphorie über die Wilson'sche Politik der Selbst-bestimmung der Völker einerseits und von verstärkter britischer Repression andererseits. In der ersten Sitzung des Dáil am 21. Januar 1919 im Dubliner Mansion House wurde die Unabhängigkeit der 'Irischen Republik' ausgerufen. Eamon de Valera, Arthur Griffith und Count Plunkett (Vater des hingerichteten Joseph Plunkett) sollten den neuen Staat auf der Pariser Friedenskonferenz vertreten. Da aber alle drei inhaftiert waren, entsandte der Dáil Sean T. O'Kelly (später Staatspräsident) und George Gavan Duffy. Am 3. Februar 1919 entkam de Valera dem Gefängnis im englischen Lincoln und wurde prompt am 1. April 1919 vom Dàil zum Präsidenten und Regierungschef gewählt. Er bildete sein erstes Kabinett - das Außenressort erhielt Count Plunkett.

Die Republik suchte umgehend internationale Anerkennung. In Paris erinnerte man sich jedoch der 'German Connection' jener Sinn Féin und IRB Leute, die jetzt in Dublin das Sagen hatten. Selbst Wilson, der Protagonist des Selbstbestimmungsrechts, war nicht besonders hilfreich. Im Juni 1919 wurde beschlossen, die irischen Abgesandten nicht zuzulassen. Nachdem London am 10. September 1919 den Dáil Éireann zur staatsgefährdenden Organisation erklärt hatte, wurden Sean O'Kelly und Gavan Duffy aus Frankreich ausgewiesen. Sie wendeten sich nach Berlin, wo sie in den Wirren jener Tage nur bei der Wirtschaft und den Freunden der Keltologie, nicht jedoch in offiziellen Kreisen Gehör fanden.

Im Februar 1921 war Gavan Duffy erneut in Berlin, dieses Mal als Sonderbotschafter des Dáil. Er traf Gustav Stresemann, der ihm aber nur die schwierige Lage des Reichs darzulegen vermochte. Die Deutsch-Irische Gesellschaft in Berlin gab für Gavan Duffy ein Abendessen, bei dem Professor Julius Pokorny eine beeindruckende Rede auf Gälisch hielt; das war aber auch alles. Die Bitte um Anerkennung der Irischen Republik war Gegenstand eines formellen Memorandums, das der Dáil im Mai 1921 dem Reichstag vorlegte. Es fruchtete nichts: die mit den Versailler Vertragsmächten ringende Weimarer Republik glaubte, Großbritannien nicht brüskieren zu können. Man erwartete bei deutschem Wohlverhalten von London Unterstützung gegen Frankreich, da es galt, die Bedingungen des Versailler Vertrags abzumildern.

In Berlin hatte das neue Irland eine beachtliche Lobby, denn schon während des Krieges hatten Casement und John Gaffney dabei geholfen, eine Deutsch-Irische Gesellschaft ins Leben zu rufen (3. Februar 1916). Zu den Vor-standsmitgliedern gehörten prominente Herren: zwei Reichs-tagsabgeordnete, der Zentrumspolitiker und Leiter der (Propaganda) Zentralstelle für den Auslandsdienst Matthias Erzberger und der Führer der Konservativen Graf Westarp sowie der Liberale Freiherr von Richthofen. Der Kaiser hatte eine für ihn typische Grußbotschaft geschickt:

"Den Freiheitskampf des tapferen Irland verfolgen seine Majestät mit Interesse und lebhafter Sympathie in dem starken Bewußtsein, daß deutsches Schwert schon eine Reihe von Völkern zur Freiheit geführt hat."

Die Deutsch-Irische Gesellschaft in Berlins Knesebeckstrasse wurde von George Chatterton-Hill und Agatha Grabisch geführt und brachte monatlich die *Irischen Blätter* heraus. Sie informierten über Irland aus Sicht der radikalen Republikaner und enthielten anti-britische Propaganda. Im Juni 1918 geriet die Gesellschaft angesichts erheblicher interner Meinungsverschiedenheiten in eine Krise. Der einflußreiche Erzberger wurde wegen seiner angeblichen "Verzichts- und Verständigungspolitik gegenüber England" aus der Gesellschaft ausgeschlossen. Der Verein dämmerte danach nur so dahin und lebte erst nach dem Krieg wieder auf.

Da Chatterton-Hill kompromittiert war, übernahm jetzt die Amerikanerin Agatha Grabisch-Bullit den Vorsitz. Sie hatte für Casement bei der Irischen Brigade gearbeitet, ihr Mann war Berater beim deutschen Generalstab gewesen. Die Gesellschaft stand zu den 'alldeutschen' Kreisen um den Historiker Dietrich Schäfer und vor allem Theodor Schiemann in enger Verbindung. Letzterer wurde zusammen mit dem Keltologen Julius Pokorny und Georg Függe Vorstandsmitglied.

Mit Hilfe der Gesellschaft öffnete ein 'Irisches Büro' seine Pforten. Im April 1921 konnte dafür Nancy Wyse-Power, eine Doktorandin des Bonner Keltologen Thurneysen, als Büroleiterin angestellt werden, auch Pokorny und sein Schüler Micheál O Briain waren formell Mitarbeiter. Das Büro sollte eine inoffizielle Botschaft sein. Der Dáil schickte im Juni 1921 daher einen ehemaligen britischen Beamten, John Chartres, der sich bis Mitte 1922 im Hotel Eden aufhielt. Im November 1921 kam Verstärkung in der Person von Charles Bewley, des späteren irischen Botschafters am Vatikan und in Berlin; er galt als Handelsexperte. Alle erreichten herzlich wenig, vor allem nicht die Anerkennung des irischen Staates. 1923 kehrten Chartres und auch Bewley enttäuscht nach Dublin zurück. Zunächst wurden beide durch Cornelius Duane ersetzt, dieser gab Ende 1923 auf dem Höhepunkt der Superinflation jedoch ebenfalls auf.

Im Gegensatz zum 'Irischen Büro', von dem nur Nancy Wyse-Power übrig blieb, bestand die Deutsch-Irische

Gesellschaft voll weiter. Sie hat es immerhin geschafft, in der Berliner Hedwigskirche am 3. August 1921 eine Gedächtnismesse für Sir Roger Casement abzuhalten und am 31. Dezember 1921 eine Trauerfeier für den verstorbenen Hungerstreiker Terence MacSwiney zu organisieren; beide Feiern waren außerordentlich gut besucht.

Die deutschen Behörden waren ob dieser irischen Aktivitäten zunehmend beunruhigt. Vom November 1921 gibt es eine Kommunikation des Auswärtigen Amtes an das Reichsinnenministerium mit der Bitte, die Aktivitäten eines Fräulein Nanzy Poviard [gemeint war sicherlich Nancy Wyse-Power], die im Berliner Hardenberg Hotel ein *Deutsches Büro für Nachrichten aus Irland* betreibe und ein Informationsblatt *Irisches Bulletin* herausgebe, zu überwachen. Was im Anschluß an diese Aufforderung geschehen ist, läßt sich nicht mehr feststellen.

ೋ

Alle irischen Bemühungen scheiterten an der Politik der Reichsregierung jener Jahre. Diese versuchte, gute Beziehungen zu England herzustellen, um sich vor der Revanche Frankreichs zu schützen und das Joch von Versailles abzuschütteln oder wenigstens zu erleichtern. London dagegen beobachtete jeden deutsch-irischen Kontakt mit größtem Argwohn. Noch im August 1921 wurde die Reichsregierung im britischen Unterhaus beschuldigt, Sinn Féin zu unterstützen, was die Deutschen verängstigt zurückwiesen.

Tatsächlich war die Beschaffung deutscher Waffen für Irland inoffiziell ein Dauerthema. Im irischen Untergrundkampf und später im Bürgerkrieg bestand großer Bedarf. Deutschland war im Versailler Vertrag Waffenhandel untersagt worden. Es mußte deshalb geschmuggelt werden, was offenbar nicht sonderlich schwierig war. Die deutsche Polizei war zwar nicht blind, glaubte zudem auch irische Kontakte zu 'bolschewistischen' Kreisen feststellen zu können, war aber beileibe nicht Versailleshörig.

Robert Briscoe, der schon vor dem Kriege gute Handelsbeziehungen zu Deutschland aufgebaut hatte,

Charles John McGuinness und Séan MacBride spielten im Waffengeschäft jener Tage die Hauptrollen. Séan MacBride war der Sohn der berühmten irischen Freiheitskämpferin Maud Gonne und des aus dem Burenkrieg bekannten John MacBride. Er sollte später (in der ersten irischen Koalitionsregierung) Außenminister, dann Vorkämpfer der Menschenrechte und Träger des Friedensnobelpreises werden.

Charles McGuinness wurde einmal in Berlin verhaftet und wegen Waffenschmuggels zu einer Geldstrafe von 2000 Reichsmark verurteilt (infolge der Inflation entsprach das aber nur noch 10 Pfund Sterling). Britische Beobachter ließen es sich nicht nehmen, beim Prozeß anwesend zu sein und protestierten ob der Milde des Urteils. Von den vielen Transaktionen ist die vom November 1921 genau bekannt: es gelangten 1500 deutsche Gewehre und 1,7 Millionen Schuß Munition aus Deutschland nach Irland.

Anfang 1922 wurde der 'Irische Freistaat' mit Dominion Status analog zu Kanada ins Leben gerufen, die 'Irische Republik' hörte auf zu existieren. Die Annahme des Minderstatus und der Teilung der Insel führte bekanntlich zum irischen Bürgerkrieg. Die Ambitionen der provisorischen irischen Regierung unter W.T. Cosgrave waren realistisch und bescheiden. Cosgrave erklärte im Rumpf-Dáil:

"Außenpolitik ist für uns, vom Außenhandel abgesehen, von keiner Bedeutung."

Der schon häufiger im Berliner Zusammenhang erwähnte Gavan Duffy, zum ersten Außenminister des Freistaats bestellt, trat wegen dieser Erklärung zurück, an seine Stelle trat Desmond Fitzgerald.

Die Gegner des Anglo-Irischen Vertrags unter Führung von Eamon de Valera scheuten sich nicht, ihre eigenen Beziehungen zu Deutschland und den USA auszubauen. Mit starker finanzieller Unterstützung aus den USA kam es in der Folgezeit immer wieder zu Waffenkäufen in Deutschland. Briscoe und McGuinness wurden auch darüber hinaus Pioniere des deutsch-irischen Handels.

Briscoe ging mit einem Berliner Handelshaus eine Partnerschaft ein. McGuinness war bald Eigner des ersten Schiffes der irischen Handelsmarine. Er nannte es bezeichnenderweise „City of Dortmund". Ferner ware der Abgeordnete Liam de Róiste zusammen mit seinem Berliner Partner Paul Funke einer der ersten, der den Handel mit Deutschland in Gang brachte.

 C୨

Auch sonst kam es - ungeachtet der fehlenden diplomatischen Beziehungen - in den 20er Jahren zu zahlreichen deutsch-irischen Kontakten. Im Juli 1922 schon bat der Vorsitzende des irischen Verfassungsausschusses - korrekterweise über die deutsche Botschaft in London - um Material über die Weimarer Verfassung. Die Weisung des Auswärtigen Amtes war eindeutig, nämlich

"jeden unmittelbaren Verkehr amtlicher Stellen mit der Vertretung des irischen Volkes vorläufig nach Möglichkeit zu vermeiden. "

Wieder einmal wurde auf die „Empfindlichkeit" der britischen Regierung in Fragen, die Irland betrafen, Rücksicht genommen. Das gewünschte Material soll jedoch seinen Adressaten auf inoffiziellem Weg erreicht haben. Eine weniger bedeutsame Episode blieb die Begegnung irischer Vertreter mit Hitler im Mai 1923, also vor dessen Marsch auf die Feldherrnhalle.

Für die Sinn Féin Politik warben im Reich unermüdlich der Schriftsteller Francis Stuart, aber auch (damals) linke IRA Leute wie Séan MacBride und Donal O'Donoghue. Diese beiden nahmen im Juli 1929 an einem Kongreß der Anti-Imperialistischen Liga in Frankfurt teil, ebenso wie das führende IRA Mitglied Peadar O'Donnell, der 1930 den Berliner Europäischen Bauernkongreß besuchte.

Im August 1927 bat der damalige Adjutant General der irischen Armee, Brennan (ebenfalls über die deutsche Botschaft in London), das Ausbildungsprogramm der Reichswehr studieren zu dürfen. Zunächst kam die gewohnte

Reaktion. Die Antwort des Truppenamtes des Reichswehrministeriums unter Leitung des späteren Reichswehrministers von Blomberg lautete:

"Abgelehnt. Zuständig ist britischer Militärattaché an der britischen Botschaft in Berlin. Im übrigen unmöglich, da alle Rheinland-Okkupationsmächte zu deutschen Truppenübungen nicht zugelassen sind."

Nach vielem Hin und Her schuf das Auswärtige Amt einen charmanten Kompromiß: Brennan durfte eine "private" Reise antreten, auf der ihn am 30. und 31. August 1927 ein Attaché (Graf Strachwitz) begleitete, ein Hauptmann der Reichswehr (von Kaufmann) zum Mittagessen einlud, um ihm anschließend in Dresden die Grenadierkaserne von einem Hauptmann Boerstling zeigen zu lassen - ein typischer Weimarer Drahtseilakt also. Keinen Erfolg hatte jedoch das irische Bemühen, für die irische Armee Stahlhelme deutschen Typs aus Deutschland geliefert zu bekommen; letztlich mußten sie nach deutschem Muster ausgerechnet in England angefertigt werden.

Unkompliziert verlief der erste Besuch de Valeras 1928 in Berlin, war er doch als Mitglied der Interparlamentarischen Union und nicht als irischer Staatsmann gekommen. Im Januar 1929 erging zum ersten Mal eine Einladung, deutsche Offiziere zur Horse Show der RDS in Dublin zu entsenden; drei Kavallerieoffiziere nahmen daran auch tatsächlich teil.

ҩ

Ein besonders erinnerungswürdiges Ereignis war der erste Überflug des Atlantik 1928 in Ost-West-Richtung, das Gegenstück zu Lindberghs West-Ost-Flug (New York - Paris, Mai 1927). Die Helden dieses gewagten Unternehmens waren Baron von Hünefeld, Kapitän Köhl und Kommandant Fitzmaurice vom Irish Air Corps. Am 12. April 1928 brachen sie von Baldonnell bei Dublin auf und landeten 36 Stunden später am 13. April auf Greenly Island in Neufundland. Die

Aktion stärkte das Selbstbewußtsein der Iren und trug nicht wenig zur Verbesserung des deutschen Ansehens bei.

Auf privater und wirtschaftlicher Ebene liefen die Kontakte also reibungslos. Sie führten dazu, daß die Zahl der Deutschen in Irland in den Zwanziger Jahren ständig wuchs, zumal der neue Staat großen Mangel an Fachkräften hatte.

Bereits im März 1923 holte General Richard Mulcahy den deutschen Oberst Fritz Brase nach Dublin, um das irische Heeresmusikwesen aufzubauen. Brase erbat sich, von Christian Sauerzweig unterstützt zu werden, und beide grün-deten die irische Armeeschule für Militärmusik. Brases *Army No. One Band* war in kürzester Zeit äußerst populär, wenige haben soviel zu einem positiven Image der Deutschen bei breiten Schichten Irlands beigetragen. Brase trat 1940 in den Ruhestand. Die Leitung der Musikschule übernahm dann sein langjähriger Vertreter Sauerzweig, bis auch er 1947 in Rente ging. Es soll nicht verschwiegen werden, daß Brase sich nach 1933 zunächst am Aufbau einer Dubliner Ortszelle der NSDAP beteiligte; von de Valera aber vor die Wahl gestellt "NSDAP oder irische Armee!" entschied sich Brase für die irische Militärmusik.

In den 20er Jahren verdankt auch das Irish National Museum seinen Aufbau zwei Deutschen, Walter Bremer und nach dessen Tod im Jahre 1927 dem Prähistoriker und Keltologen Dr. Adolf Mahr. Von Aloys Fleischmann, der 1972 in Cork starb, war schon in anderem Zusammenhang die Rede. Seine Verdienste um die Musik in Irland sind bis heute unvergessen, vor allem auch, weil sein 1995 verstorbener Sohn die Arbeit weiterführte.

Kulturschaffend, wenn auch umstritten, könnte man auch W. Paffrath nennen, der über Jahrzehnte in seiner Manufaktur zahllose Gipsfiguren von Madonnen und Heiligen herstellte. Die katholischen Kirchen Irlands sind bis heute voll davon. Die (hohlen) Gipsfiguren sollen sich übrigens hervorragend zum Schmuggeln von Whiskey von Nordirland in die Republik geeignet haben. Heinrich Böll hat diesem Werk in seinem Tagebuch ein Denkmal gesetzt. Er schreibt,

*"daß einige Leute in Irland viel Geld an Gipsfiguren
verdienen müssen - ich hörte, einer davon sei ein
Deutscher, der so die Segnungen deutscher Kultur
über Irland ausbreitet."*

Auch im wirtschaftlichen Bereich sind Verdienste zu
nennen: Dr. Mecking half bei der Gründung der Irischen
Torfgesellschaft Bord na Mona mit und organisierte den
staatlichen Torfabbau. Dr. Reinhart schuf die Grundlagen
einer ordentlichen staatlichen Forstwirtschaft. Im industriellen
Bereich seien erwähnt: Dr. Winkelmann, der die Irish Glass
Bottle Factory wiederbelebte; F. Schubert, der das gleiche für
die Glühbirnenfabrik Solus tat; Georg Fäsenfeld, der die von
Sean Lemass gegründete Fleischfabrik in Roscrea moder-
nisierte, bis er auf britischen Druck hin während des 2. Weltkriegs aufgeben mußte. Er wechselte zur irischen Pharmazie
über.

Ein ganz besonderer und einmaliger Beitrag zur
Festigung der deutsch-irischen Beziehungen stellte der Bau
des hydro-elektrischen Kraftwerks in Ardnacrusha am
Shannon dar. Es brachte einen wesentlichen Moderni-
sierungsschub im immer noch vorwiegend landwirtschaft-
lichen Irland. Mit diesem Kraftwerk wurde die Elektrifizierung
des ganzen Landes eingeleitet. Der Plan für Ardnacrusha
stammte vom irischen Physiker Thomas McLaughlin, der
zunächst in Galway lehrte, dann aber als Ingenieur bei
Siemens in Berlin Arbeit fand. (Er war später langjähriger
Chef der irischen Elektrizitätswerke ESB).

Wie so häufig war es eine persönliche Verbindung,
die den Startschuß ermöglichte. Der Industrie- und Handels-
minister des Jahres 1921, Thomas McGilligan, war ein
Studienfreund McLaughlins und ließ sich von dessen Plan
überzeugen. Das Projekt wurde in Norwegen, Schweden,
Schweiz und Deutschland (nicht aber in Großbritannien)
ausgeschrieben. Die Firma Siemens-Schuckert erhielt den
Zuschlag. Die Kosten wurden auf 5,2 Millionen Pfund
veranschlagt. Wie mutig die keineswegs unumstrittene
Entscheidung war, zeigt die Tatsache, daß das gesamte
Budget des irischen Freistaates insgesamt nur 25 Millionen
Pfund ausmachte. Am 13. August 1925 wurde der Vertrag

abgeschlossen. Der Segen des Bischofs von Killaloe, Dr. Fogarty, durfte nicht fehlen. Nach 3½ Jahren konnten am 22. Juli 1929 die Schleusen geöffnet werden. Das Projekt brachte nicht nur über 300 deutsche Ingenieure und Techniker für viele Jahre ins Shannongebiet, sondern hatte auch einen enormen Ausbildungseffekt.

Das deutsche Image wurde landesweit neu geprägt, da die deutschen Techniker im ganzen Land Transformatoren und Umspannungsstationen aufzubauen sowie 2000 km Leitungen zu verlegen hatten. Zahlreiche Freundschaften, darunter auch deutsch-irische Ehen, waren ein Nebeneffekt des Projekts. Es konnte aber nicht ausbleiben, daß es auch Stimmen gab, die von der Gefahr der Überfremdung sprachen.

Das Shannon Projekt beeinflußte natürlich auch die deutsch-irische Handelsbilanz erheblich, und sie war stark unausgeglichen. Die Einfuhren aus Deutschland stiegen bis 1930 auf £1.329.931 (1924: £744.580), während die Ausfuhren nach Deutschland £237.981 betrugen.

ରଙ

Der erste offizielle Vertrag zwischen beiden Ländern war der deutsch-irische Handels- und Schiffahrtsvertrag vom Mai 1930, der erste Vertrag dieser Art, den der Freistaat überhaupt abschloß. Der Handel hatte für Irland erste Priorität. Die irische Industrial Development Agency (IDA) und viele irische Kaufleute waren regelmäßige Besucher der Leipziger Messe. So wurde Deutschland allmählich wichtigster irischer Handelspartner außerhalb des Commonwealth und rangierte an zweiter Stelle hinter Großbritannien.

In Berlin war man erleichtert darüber, daß der Freistaat sehr bald auf seinen Anteil an deutschen Reparationszahlungen verzichtete. Auch später zeigte sich die äußerst wohlwollende irische Haltung: de Valera äußerte bald nach seinem Regierungsantritt die Auffassung, daß die Versailler Reparationsauflagen Deutschlands völlig gestrichen werden sollten.

Diplomatische Beziehungen zwischen den beiden Ländern kamen erst nach 1929 zustande. Als 'Dominion' im britischen Commonwealth mußte sich Irland bis 1929 offiziell in Berlin durch die britische Botschaft vertreten lassen. Erst dann wurde der Status als Dominion modifiziert und zwar dahingehend, daß separate diplomatische Beziehungen möglich waren.

Immerhin gab es seit 1923 konsularische Beziehungen. Im November 1923 hatte das Reich in Dublin ein Generalkonsulat eröffnet. Der erste Generalkonsul, Dr. Georg von Dehn-Schmidt, hatte davor als Konsul von Liverpool aus die irischen Angelegenheiten wahrgenommen. Bis 1934 sollte er die Interessen des Reichs in Dublin vertreten. In diesem Zusammenhang zeigt übrigens ein Brief, den der bayerische Ministerpräsident Hugo Graf Lerchenfeld am 4. April 1922 an Außenminister Walther Rathenau richtete, was man sich bei der Sache dachte. Lerchenfeld schrieb:

"Wichtig erscheint mir auch die Besetzung unseres Generalkonsulats in Dublin mit einem namhaften deutschen Katholiken. [...] Die Pflege der Beziehungen zwischen Deutschland und Irland unter Ausnutzung des katholischen Elements verspricht gute Früchte."

1930 wurde in Berlin eine irische Gesandtschaft gegründet. Erster Gesandter war Professor Daniel A. Binchy, ein Gelehrter hohen Ansehens, der gut Deutsch sprach, über die irischen Benediktiner in Regensburg promoviert hatte und schon im Alter von 24 Jahren zum Professor für Recht am Trinity College Dublin ernannt worden war. Für den Rechtsstatus Irlands bezeichnend war sein Beglaubigungsschreiben. Es begann mit der Formel: *"S.M., der König des Vereinigten Königreichs von Großbritannien und Irland und der Britischen Dominion Übersee , Kaiser von Indien ..."*

Binchy, obgleich in Berlin hochgeschätzt, fühlte sich in der neuen Rolle nicht sehr wohl und kehrte 1932 in die akademische Laufbahn zurück. Eine Anekdote berichtet, daß er beim Termin zur Überreichung seines Beglaubigungsschreibens erst im Vorzimmer von Präsident Hindenburg merkte, daß er das Dokument im Hotel vergessen hatte. Es mußte in einer Eilaktion herbeigeschafft werden.

Im Gleichklang mit dem Aufbau der irischen Vertretung in Berlin wurde 1930 das deutsche Generalkonsulat in Dublin zur Gesandtschaft angehoben. Georg von Dehn-Schmidt erhielt den Rang eines Gesandten. Die deutsche Bürokratie ließ sich dabei etwas Zeit, so daß die irische Regierung unter Druck geriet, da man in Dublin entschlossen war, die deutsche Gesandtschaft vor der französischen errichtet zu sehen. Während in Berlin der Amtsschimmel schlief, waren die Franzosen längst zur Eröffnung einer Gesandtschaft in Dublin bereit. Dublin mahnte zur Eile, und bald nach der Formalisierung der Beziehungen lud die Reichsregierung den irischen Außenminister, Patrick McGilligan, dessen Gattin und seinen Staatssekretär, Joseph Walshe, nach Berlin ein. Der Besuch fand vom 26. bis 29. Mai 1931 statt; zu dem üblichen Gegenbesuch Reichskanzler Brünings und Außenminister Curtius' kam es infolge der Turbulenzen der Weimarer Endzeit allerdings nicht mehr.

6. De Valera und das Dritte Reich

Die Weltwirtschaftskrise von 1929 hat in beiden Ländern wesentliche Veränderungen ausgelöst; an dieser Stelle empfiehlt sich abermals eine allgemeine Lagebeschreibung. In Irland wie in anderen europäischen Ländern gab es häufig Zweifel, ob man der Schwierigkeiten mit den überkommenen demokratischen Institutionen Herr werden könne. Der Faschismus in Italien erschien manchem als ein interessantes Experiment, zumal die katholische Kirche ihm zunächst keineswegs ablehnend gegenüber stand. Im Februar 1932 ging Fianna Fáil siegreich aus den Wahlen hervor. Diese Partei war von de Valera, dem ehemaligen Gegner des anglo-irischen Vertrags, im Mai 1926 gegründet worden; seinen zunächst praktizierten Boykott des irischen Parlaments hatte dieser aber im August 1927 aufgegeben. Das führte zur Spaltung der radikalen republikanischen Bewegung in einen konstitutionellen und in einen weiterhin radikalen Teil. Die neue Regierung de Valeras löste die zur Erfüllung des anglo-irischen Vertrags entschlossene Regierung Cosgrave ab, an deren freihändlerischem Kurs allgemein Zweifel entstanden waren. De Valera propagierte einen ökonomischen Nationalismus, dessen Kernstück eine strikte Schutzzollpolitik und das Streben nach weitgehender Autarkie war. Die mit England vereinbarten Entschädigungszahlungen wurden eingestellt. London reagierte mit Anhebung der Zölle für irische Produkte, ein Handelskrieg brach aus, der bis 1938 dauern sollte und die irische Wirtschaft schwer belastete.

De Valera ergriff weitere umwälzende Maßnahmen: der Eid auf die britische Krone und das Amt des britischen Generalgouverneurs wurden abgeschafft. Das ganze anglo-irische Vertragswerk von 1921/22 wurde schrittweise abgebaut, bis es 1938 zu einer Bereinigung des irisch-britischen Verhältnisses kam, in der sogar die irischen Vertrags-häfen von England zurückgegeben wurden. Besonders Sturm (1984, s. Literaturverzeichnis) hat die starken Parallelen aufgezeigt, die in den Jahren unmittelbar nach 1933 zwischen Deutschland und Irland bestanden. Für beide Länder galten folgende Feststellungen: ein Regimewechsel fand statt, zu dem nicht unerheblich die Weltwirtschaftskrise beigetragen hatte; gesteigerter Patriotismus und nationales Selbstwertgefühl prägten die Atmosphäre ebenso wie die Überzeugung vieler von der Höherwertigkeit des nationalen Erbes und der eigenen Kultur.

Die Opposition gegen ein als ungerecht empfundenes internationales Vertragswerk (Anglo-Irischer/Versailler Vertrag) war übermächtig geworden und hatte sich zum Ziel gesetzt, dieses zu revidieren, zu unterlaufen oder nicht zu erfüllen.

Die sozialistischen Ideen und erst recht der Kommunismus wurden abgelehnt. Ebenso wurde der Liberalismus für gescheitert erklärt. Nationalismus, verbunden mit weitgehenden staatlichen Sozialprogrammen, schien die Lösung der Probleme. Ein Sieg des Kommunismus galt als extreme Gefahr, ein autoritärer Führungsstil hingegen wurde als das kleinere Übel akzeptiert.

Hier enden jedoch die Parallelen; denn im Gegensatz zu Deutschland galten in Irland die parlamentarische Demokratie und ihre Institutionen als das unverzichtbare Ergebnis des jahrhundertelangen Kampfes um Unabhängigkeit. De Valera hatte zwar einen autoritären Führungsstil, aber er spielte nach demokratischen Regeln und bediente sich demokratischer Institutionen. Er fühlte sich zum Lager der westlichen Demokratien gehörig; seine ideologische Basis war nicht purer Nationalismus oder gar Rassenwahn, sondern sein streng katholischer Glaube.

Die Einstellung der Iren zum Deutschland nach Hitlers Machtübernahme war ambivalent. Von wenigen überzeugten Faschisten abgesehen, die sich aber eher an Mussolini als an Hitler ein Vorbild nahmen, war man in Irland kein Freund der Nationalsozialisten. Manche Iren hatten zunächst Verständnis für die autoritären Regime auf dem Kontinent, und dazu zählten wohl auch prominente Personen wie der

Staatssekretär im Außenamt von 1922-1946, Joseph Walshe (später irischer Botschafter beim Vatikan) und William Butler Yeats, der sich daher auch nicht scheute, 1934 in Frankfurt die Goethe-Medaille anzunehmen. Die Sympathie für das Hitlerregime schwand aber in dem Maß, in dem die Kirchenpolitik der NSDAP offenkundig wurde.

ભ

Es gab die Bewegung 'Irischer Blauhemden' (National Guard), die in ihrem Gebaren die Faschisten imitierten. Diese Organisation rekrutierte sich vorwiegend aus der Opposition der irischen Landwirte, die durch den irisch-britischen Handelskrieg wirtschaftlich schwer getroffen waren. Ihr Führer war General Eoin O'Duffy. Die Blauhemden waren jedoch nie eine anti-konfessionelle Bewegung wie SS, SA oder die Hitlerjugend. Die Organisation der Blauhemden vermochte noch 1936 eine irische Brigade für den spanischen Bürgerkrieg zur Unterstützung Francos zusammenzustellen, führte danach aber nur noch ein Schattendasein. Der Plan einer 'Grünen Division' zum Kampf an der Seite Hitlers 'gegen den Bolschewismus' blieb in den ersten Anfängen stecken.

Die fast militante anti-kommunistische Haltung der überwiegenden Mehrheit der Iren im katholischen Staat de Valeras liefert die Erklärung für so manchen irischen Vorgang jener Vorkriegsjahre, der von Außenstehenden als faschistisch oder sogar nazistisch interpretiert wurde. Kommunistisch war identisch mit atheistisch, und das war für alle Iren - ein paar Intellektuelle ausgenommen - völlig unirisch. Auch der vorherrschende latente Anti-Semitismus hatte keine rassenideologischen, sondern hauptsächlich kirchliche Wurzeln. Er war auch weniger eine Anti-Haltung, eher das Fehlen von Sympathie und das Bedürfnis nach gesellschaft-licher und konfessioneller Homogenität.

Politisch brachten die Vorkriegsjahre keine besondere Annäherung zwischen Deutschland und Irland. Wohl aber wuchs die wirtschaftliche Bedeutung des Reiches für Irland infolge des irisch-britischen Handelskriegs. Die irische Regierung bemühte sich ab 1932 sehr, zu einer engeren

Wirtschaftskooperation zu kommen. Sie bot beispielsweise an, ein zweites Wasserkraftwerk (an der Liffey) aus Deutschland zu beziehen, in Kombination mit umfangreichen langfristigen deutschen Kohlelieferungen. Die deutsche Reaktion war jedoch zunächst kühl; erneut bemühte man sich in Berlin, dieses Mal unter Nazivorzeichen, um ein gutes Verhältnis zu England, der 'arisch reinrassigen germanischen Brudernation'. Es kam zu keiner spektakulären Zusammenarbeit, wie die Iren - im Handelskrieg mit Großbritannien - sich das wünschten. Einige kleinere Projekte kamen zustande, so zum Beispiel die Hilfe beim Ausbau der irischen Zuckerindustrie, bei der Energiegewinnung durch Torf, bei der Verwendung einer weiteren Turbine im Shannon-Kraftwerk. Erst die Erkenntnis der enormen Devisenknappheit des Reiches 1934/35 zwang Berlin zu einer dynamischeren Sicht des deutschen Außenhandels. So kam es im Januar 1935 zu einem deutsch-irischen Handelsvertrag, in dem das Verhältnis von Einfuhren zu Ausfuhren mit 3:1 festgelegt wurde. Diese Relation wurde im Februar 1936 auf 2:1 und Ende 1936 auf 3:2 angehoben. Im Vordergrund standen irische landwirtschaftliche Produkte. Zwischen 1933 und 1938 stiegen die irischen Ausfuhren von £66.408 auf £912.269 an, die Einfuhren aus Deutschland verbesserten sich von £1,3 auf £1,5 Millionen; dennoch, und trotz des Handelskriegs, blieb das Reich an zweiter Stelle hinter Großbritannien.

∽

In den rein diplomatischen Beziehungen veränderte sich in der Vorkriegszeit wenig. Der Gesandte von Dehn-Schmidt, der seit 1923 in Dublin die Reichsregierung vertrat, wurde 1934 als Leiter der Gesandtschaft nach Bukarest versetzt. In Dublin erlebte er noch am 28. März 1933 die ersten Protestkundgebungen gegen die Behandlung der Juden im Nazi-Deutschland. Sie wurden vom Dubliner Oberrabiner Dr. Isaac Herzog, dem Vater des späteren israelischen Staatspräsidenten Chaim Herzog, angeführt und von von Dehn-Schmidt als Karrierediplomat pflichtgemäß berichtet.

Ob von Dehn-Schmidt in Irland während seines elfjährigen Aufenthalts beliebt war oder nicht, ist in der Literatur umstritten und kaum nachprüfbar. Er war wohl wie die meisten seiner deutschen Kollegen kein Gegner der nationalen Aufbruchstimmung im Reich, was nicht notwendigerweise mit Nazisympathien gleichzusetzen war. In Irland verfügte er über gute Kontakte; nachhaltige Wirkung hatte vor allem seine Freundschaft mit dem Herausgeber der Irish Times, Robert M. Smyllie, einem interessierten und wohlwollenden Beobachter der deutschen Szene. Smyllie hat zwei viel beachtete Bücher über Deutschland geschrieben: *A New Germany* (1929) und *Germany Under Adolf Hitler* (1936).

Wie immer von Dehn-Schmidt zu beurteilen ist, die Behandlung, die er nach seiner Zeit in Dublin zu Hause erfuhr, hatte er nicht verdient. Eine für die Nazi-Zeit bezeichnende Geschichte: von Dehn-Schmidt verabschiedete sich in Dublin im Herbst 1934 in der gehörigen Form, und dazu zählte auch ein Besuch beim Doyen des diplomatischen Corps, dem apostolischen Nuntius. Wie keineswegs unüblich, küßte der scheidende deutsche Gesandte dem Nuntius im Rang eines Erzbischofs den Ring. Ein Photo dieser traditionellen Geste wurde der Nazi-Zeitung "Völkischer Beobachter" zugespielt. Hitler und die NSDAP waren empört, 'das sei ein unwürdiges Verhalten für einen aufrechten arischen Deutschen', und eine Pressekampagne gegen ihn setzte ein. Von Dehn-Schmidt, der am 8. November 1934 die Geschäfte in Bukarest bereits übernommen hatte, wurde gegen seinen Willen am 22. Februar 1935 in den einstweiligen und am 22. November 1935 in den endgültigen Ruhestand versetzt und starb verbittert im Juli 1937 in München. Sein Freund Robert Smyllie war bei seiner Beerdigung.

Irischerseits hatte der Gesandte D.A. Binchy die irische Gesandtschaft in Berlin, Drakestraße 3, schon 1932 verlassen. Ein recht kritischer Artikel über Hitler in der irischen Presse vom März 1933 zeugte von Binchys Weitblick und Integrität. Seine Rückkehr ins Reich war danach jedoch nicht mehr erwünscht. Erst im Sommer 1933 trat sein Nachfolger, der bereits für das Jahr 1922 genannte Charles Bewley, den Dienst an. Anders als Binchy war Bewley ein vorbehaltloser Bewunderer des Dritten Reiches. Seine einseitige Sicht der Dinge war notorisch, auch in Dublin. Es verwundert rückblickend, daß es erst 1937 im Dáil Éireann zu einer Anfrage in dieser Hinsicht kam. Allerlei Reibereien mit der irischen Regierung führten schließlich 1938 zu Bewleys Abberufung und Entlassung. Er zog nach Rom, ins Land Mussolinis, wo er einmal Botschafter beim Vatikan gewesen war. Erst 1962 trat Bewley noch einmal hervor, als er in den USA ein Buch *Hermann Göring und das Dritte Reich* mit Dokumenten der Familie Göring veröffentlichte.

Die Ernennung eines neuen irischen Botschafters in Berlin verzögerte sich und wurde vom Kriegsbeginn 1939 überholt. Der Krieg Deutschlands mit England machte es Irland unmöglich, den Posten zu besetzten, da man hierzu die Unterschrift des britischen Königs benötigt hätte. Der Dominionstatus des Landes, die Mitwirkung der britischen Krone also, wäre übrigens auch zur Erteilung des Agréments für einen neuen deutschen Gesandten erforderlich gewesen, eine Tatsache, die später Hempels Abberufung entgegenstand. Vorgesehen für die Nachfolge Bewleys war Dr. Thomas Joseph (Tom) Kiernan, der mit der Sängerin Delia Murphy, der 'Amsel der irischen Balladen' verheiratet war. Er wurde erst nach dem Krieg Botschafter in Deutschland.

Ab 1938 bis Juni 1942 leitete William Warnock als Geschäftsträger die irische Gesandtschaft in Berlin. Als es ihm gelang, 1942 auf Heimaturlaub in Irland zu bleiben, übernahm der bisherige Vertreter Irlands in Vichy, Cornelius Cremin, die Geschäfte bis zum Ende des Krieges.

Nachfolger von Dehn-Schmidts wurde im Oktober 1934 ein weiterer Karrierediplomat, Wilhelm von Kuhlmann. Für die damaligen Verhältnisse bezeichnend ist folgende Anekdote: als von Kuhlmann im Hafen von Cobh von Bord ging, wurde er von einem hohen Beamten des irischen Außenamtes mit 'Heil Hitler!' begrüßt. Wie die Irish Times vom 25. Oktober 1937 verbrieft, spielte eine Militärkapelle nicht nur das Deutschlandlied, sondern auch das Horst-Wessel-Lied, die wohlbekannte Hymne der Nazis, von der Zeitung keineswegs ironisch "die alte und die neue deutsche Nationalhymne" genannt - schließlich war die Militärmusik in der Regie von Oberst Fritz Brase. Von Kuhlmanns Aufenthalt in Dublin war von persönlichem Unglück gezeichnet. Seine Mutter kam in einem Feuer in seinem Haus in Cabinteely ums Leben. Er selbst war meist krank und starb schon 1937.

Die Ankunft von Kuhlmanns in Dublin verlief nicht ohne Zwischenfälle. Als es um das Schicksal des deutschen Kommunistenführers Thälmann ging, wurde das Kanzlei-gebäude der Gesandtschaft in der Northumberland Road mit der Parole "Heraus mit Thälmann" beschmiert. Auf dem Weg zum irischen Staatspräsidenten konnte von Kuhlmann im Phoenix Park die Banner kaum übersehen, auf denen stand: "Free Thälmann! Down with Hitler!"

Nach von Kuhlmanns Tod übernahm Dr. Eduard Hempel die Gesandtschaft. Als er 1937 seinen Dienst antrat, hat er es sich wohl nicht träumen lassen, daß er die Grüne Insel erst zwölf Jahre später wieder verlassen würde. Hempel war sicherlich national gesinnt, aber kein militanter Nazi. Umstritten ist, wie er 1937 Leiter einer Auslandsvertretung des Dritten Reiches hat werden können, besonders angesichts der Tatsache, daß die Besetzung solcher Posten der Zustimmung der Auslandsorganisation der NSDAP bedurfte. Das Gerücht, Frau Hempel habe die Beziehungen zu einem Verwandten spielen lassen, der Träger des NS Blutordens gewesen sei, wurde von ihr jedoch später bestritten.

Hempel hatte von Anfang an einen schweren Stand. Von Kriegsbeginn an waren die Probleme der Vertretung so, daß es unmöglich war, nur *bona figura* zu machen und "Gott einen guten Mann, und die in Berlin gute Leute sein zu lassen", selbst wenn Hempel das wirklich gewollt hätte. Hempel war umringt von Neidern, Scharfmachern und Aufpassern aus verschiedenen NS-Kreisen: Leuten des Fichtebundes, der Auslandsorganisation der Nazi Partei (AO) unter Gauleiter Bohle, der Ortsgruppe der NSDAP, der ver-schiedenen deutschen Geheimdienste. Selbst sein Ständiger Vertreter, Legationsrat Henning Thomsen, war SS-Mann.

Damit soll nicht gesagt werden, daß es Anzeichen gab, wonach Hempel sich je versucht fühlte, die Grenzen der Loyalität zur Reichsregierung oder zum Führer zu testen.

Das Umfeld der deutschen NS-Sympathisanten im Irland jener Tage ist leicht zu begreifen. Fern von den bedrückenden täglichen Auswirkungen des NS Regimes in der Heimat befanden sich die Irlanddeutschen (1936 insgesamt 526 Personen) in einer Atmosphäre, die von irischem Nationalismus und anti-britischen Gefühlen geprägt war. Viele Iren waren mit Hitlers Regime nicht einverstanden. Wenn sie jedoch an den verhaßten großen Nachbarn und ihre nationale Bestrebung dachten, die Teilung der Insel zu überwinden, schien ihnen deutsche Hilfe als etwas, was sie nicht ablehnen sollten. Es wundert nicht, daß sich die deutsche Kolonie ungeniert deutsch-nationalistisch gab und dabei viele irische Freunde haben konnte.

Eine Ortsgruppe der NSDAP war bereits im Mai 1934 gegründet worden. Nachdem Oberst Brase die Leitung der Gruppe abgab, übernahm Adolf Mahr, der Direktor des Irischen Nationalmuseums, die Aufgabe. Aber auch er mußte als irischer Staatsangestellter 1938 das Amt abgeben. Unter den Deutschen lief nicht alles nur auf der Parteischiene. 1934 wurde auch eine "Deutsche Vereinigung" geschaffen, deren Vorstand die Firmenvertreter von Siemens-Schuckert und AEG, Müller-Dubrow und Karl Krause, übernahmen. Man traf sich im Red Bank Restaurant in der D'Olier Street von Dublin. 1935 hatte dieser deutsche Club immerhin 120 Mitglieder, die NSDAP Ortsgruppe hingegen nur 31.

CR

Eine größere jüdische oder sonstige politische Flüchtlingsgemeinde existierte bei Kriegsbeginn in Irland nicht. Die Einwanderungspolitik der Regierung de Valera war äußerst restriktiv (im ganzen Land gab es laut irischer Volkszählung im Jahre 1936 nur 3649 Bürger jüdischen Glaubens). Bis 1939 sollen etwa 90 deutsche und österreichische Juden eine vorübergehende Aufenthaltserlaubnis erhalten haben, im Dezember 1939 wurden zusätzlich noch zwanzig 'christianisierte' (d.h. getaufte) Juden aus Hamburg aufgenommen. Dazu kamen 1940 noch vierzig weitere Flüchtlinge. Die Art, mit der Botschafter Bewley in Berlin die

Visa-Anträge behandelte (oder besser, nicht behandelte) spielte bei dieser Ablehnungspolitik eine große Rolle. Die meisten Flüchtlinge in Irland konnten aber nur mit Mühe ihr Auskommen finden, da sie mit wenigen Ausnahmen alle Akademiker waren, deren deutsche Diplome nicht automatisch anerkannt wurden. Zu diesen zählten Ärzte wie z. B. Dr. R.A. Neumann aus Berlin, der spätere Vertrauensarzt fast aller westeuropäischen Botschaften und dessen Frau Dr. Marianne Neumann (ebenfalls Ärztin), welche die Tradition ihres Mannes noch bis zum heutigen Tag weiterführt. Beide mußten ihre Examen 'nachmachen'. Ebenso erging es Professor Sachs, der sich in der Medizingeschichte um die Bestimmung der Blutgruppen verdient gemacht hat, oder Geisteswissenschaftlern wie Professor Lewy und Dr. Ernst Schyer.

CR

Am 11. September 1939 verließen 33 deutsche Staatsangehörige, meist wehrpflichtige Männer, die Grüne Insel in Richtung Reich. Darunter waren Dr. Hellmut Clissmann (Universitätslektor und Vertreter des Deutschen Akademischen Austauschdienstes/DAAD), Dr. Adolf Mahr (Direktor des Irischen Nationalmuseums), Müller-Dubrow (Siemens), der Keltologe Ludwig Mühlhausen, die Universitätslektoren Helmut Bauersfeld und Hans Hartmann. Fast alle wurden zu Hause zum Militär eingezogen und/oder "Sonderverwendungen" in Sachen Irland zugeführt. Clissmann wurde so zunächst der Gesandtschaft in Kopenhagen, dann als Soldat der militärischen Abwehr (Canaris) in Berlin zugeteilt. Mahr kam zunächst in der Kulturabteilung des Auswärtigen Amt unter, Mühlhausen wurde Ordinarius für Keltologie, führendes Mitglied des NS-Dozentenbundes, als SS-Mann Leiter der 'keltischen Arbeitsgruppe im Kriegseinsatz der Geisteswissenschaften' und schließlich SD-Mitarbeiter in der Bretagne.

Zu den Sondereinsätzen 'Irland' zählte vor allem die Arbeit für Goebbels' Propagandaministerium, das regelmäßige Rundfunksendungen auch für England und Irland ausstrahlen ließ. Bauersfeld und Hartmann wurden hier als Redakteure eingesetzt.

Führende Mitarbeiter des Senders waren William Joyce, bekannt als *Lord Haw-Haw*, und der bekannte Schriftsteller Francis Stuart. Dieser war schon vor dem Krieg Universitätslektor in Berlin gewesen und war während eines Urlaubs in Irland vom Kriegsbeginn überrascht worden. Mit finanzieller Hilfe Hempels und der Unterstützung des DAAD gelang es ihm unter Mühen, im Januar 1940 nach Berlin zurückzukehren, wo er glaubte, der nationalistischen irischen Sache am besten dienen zu können.

William Joyce war eine eher abenteuerliche Figur. In New York geboren, gesellte er sich zunächst zum britischen Faschistenführer Sir Oswald Mosley, um nach einem Streit mit diesem seine eigene nationalsozialistische Partei zu gründen. Dabei scheiterte er und begab sich nach Berlin. Unter falschen Angaben hatte er die britische Staatsangehörigkeit erworben, was ihm schließlich zum Verhängnis werden sollte. Dieser britische Paß wurde zwar 1940 ungültig, deshalb beanspruchte er nach 1945, Amerikaner und nicht Brite zu sein. Die neun Monate von Kriegsbeginn bis Ablauf seines britischen Passes genügten aber, um Joyce nach dem Krieg wegen Landesverrats nach britischem Recht zum Tode zu verurteilen und hinzurichten.

Verhängnisvoll war, daß das Dritte Reich seine Irlandpolitik in erster Linie auf den Informationen und Bewertungen dieses in Deutschland weilenden Personenkreises von 'Rückkehrern' und 'expatriates' aufbaute. Das führte wiederholt zu einer einseitigen und falschen Einschätzung der Lage in Irland, was eine Episode vom Februar 1939 zeigt: Als Oskar Pfaus, der Vertreter des NS-Fichtebundes (eine alldeutsche Gründung des 1. Weltkriegs und nach 1933 ein Goebbels'sches Instrument der NS-Propaganda) in Dublin auftauchte, nahm er sofort Kontakt mit Eoin O'Duffy, dem Führer der bereits marginalisierten irischen 'Blauhemden' auf, um diesen zu veranlassen, ihn (Pfaus) in die Führungsebene der IRA einzuführen. Pfaus hätte wissen sollen, daß die IRA zu O'Duffys Erzfeinden zählte.

Pfaus schaffte es dennoch, auf anderem Weg zum IRA Führer Séan Russell vorzudringen. In der Tat folgte aus dieser Begegnung, daß Séan Russells engster Kampfgefährte, der IRA Mann Seamus (Jim) O'Donovan, kurze Zeit darauf nach Deutschland geschickt wurde, und zwar mit dem Auftrag, die Kampagne der IRA mit den deutschen Stellen zu koordinieren. Auch das war in hohem Maße naiv und uninformiert, wie noch zu zeigen sein wird. Der Fichtebund ließ sich im übrigen auch lange Zeit nicht davon abbringen, Propagandamaterial der Nazis über England nach Irland zu schicken, welches meistens abgefangen wurde und obendrein die irischen Adressaten diskreditierte.

Auf der irischen Seite läßt sich so manche Reaktion jener Jahre nur mit Unkenntnis und Haß auf alles Britische erklären. Die alte Devise 'Englands Schwierigkeiten sind Irlands Chance' galt noch immer. Dabei unterschied sich die leicht pro-deutsche Stimmung auf dem irischen Lande von der eher kritischen Haltung der aufgeklärteren Medien und der Intellektuellen in den Städten. Aber auch auf dem Lande wandelte sich die Einstellung in dem Maß, in dem das Nazi Regime gegen die katholische Kirche in Deutschland vorging und diese Tatsache in Irland bekannt wurde.

7. Erneut Krieg

Der 2.Weltkrieg eröffnete ein neues Kapitel der deutsch-irischen Beziehungen, und zum ersten Mal erhielten diese einen hochpolitischen Charakter. Berlins und Hempels Sorge war hauptsächlich, ob Irland neutral bleiben wolle und könne. Unmittelbar nach Kriegsausbruch hatte Reichsaußenminister von Ribbentrop via Hempel Präsident de Valera wissen lassen, das Reich werde sich feindlicher Aktionen gegen irisches Territorium enthalten, vorausgesetzt, Irland beachte 'unimpeachable' (einwandfreie) Neutralität. Der Ausdruck 'unimpeachable' mißfiel de Valera. Er ließ Hempel wissen, Irland werde - seiner wirtschaftlichen Abhängigkeit von Großbritannien und der Gefahr britischer Intervention in Irland wegen - nicht umhinkönnen, gewisse Rücksichten auf England zu nehmen. Er verbitte sich aber von beiden Kriegsparteien dreierlei: die Verletzung des irischen Bodens und der irischen Gewässer, die Ausnutzung der irischen nationalistischen Bewegung zu anti-britischen Aktionen sowie feindliche Akte gegen die Menschen auf beiden Seiten der Grenze zu Nordirland.

De Valera war fest zur Neutralität entschlossen, koste es was es wolle. Er erklärte im März 1941 emphatisch:

> "Jahrhundertelanger Anstrengungen hat es bedurft, um die irische Unabhängigkeit zu gewinnen. Wir sind entschlossen, sie nicht wieder verloren gehen zu lassen."

Hempels Lagebeurteilung vor und zu Beginn des Krieges war, daß Irland auf Dauer schwerlich werde neutral bleiben können. Der nationale Notstand ('Emergency'), den das Parlament ausrief und die außerordentlichen Vollmachten, die de Valera erhielt, verbesserten dessen

Chancen, seine Neutralitätspolitik auch gegen Opposition im Dáil durchzuhalten. In den ersten Monaten des Krieges war es für die Iren keineswegs sicher, daß Großbritannien nicht die irische Republik besetzen und sich der ganzen Insel als Flankenschutz bedienen werde. Insbesondere die Nutzung der hervorragenden irischen Häfen Cobh, Berehaven und Lough Swilly - England bereute, diese 1937 zurückgegeben zu haben - war eine ständige britische Forderung; de Valera blieb jedoch hart und gab ihr nicht nach.

Mit dem Beginn der deutschen Kampagne gegen England (Operation 'Seelöwe') trat an die Stelle der Furcht vor einer britischen Invasion die vor einer deutschen. Vor allem die deutsche Besetzung Belgiens und der Niederlande konsternierte viele Iren, viel Sympathie für Deutschland ging damit verloren. Im August 1940 erhielt Hempel (auf seine dringenden Bitten hin) endlich von Ribbentrop die Weisung, de Valera zu sagen, daß "*alle beteiligten [deutschen] Stellen strikte Anweisung haben, bei Unternehmungen irgendwelcher Art gegen England nicht Irland als Ausgangspunkt zu nehmen*". Die Invasionsangst wurde dadurch etwas abge-mildert.

CR

Besonders aktuell war ab Anfang 1940 die Frage, ob das Reich in seine Blockade gegen England auch Irland ein-beziehen werde. Für die ohnehin angespannte Versorgungs-lage der Insel war dies von erheblicher Bedeutung. Formal gesehen fand eine solche Blockade zwar nicht statt. Die deutsche Marine versenkte aber immer wieder "aus Ver-sehen" irische Frachtschiffe, erstmals im September 1939 im Falle der *Inver Liffey*, im Februar 1940 mit der *Munster,* einem 43.000 Tonnen Frachter. Andere Schiffe folgten dann bis ins Jahr 1944. So wurden beispielsweise am 2. Juni 1942 die *City of Bremen*, am 15. Mai 1943 die *Irish Oak* versenkt. Im April 1941 protestierte die irische Regierung wegen der Versenkung von drei irischen Frachtern (die *Glencullen*, die *Glencree,* und die *Edenvale*), die für die Versorgung Irlands mit Kohle lebenswichtig waren: alle waren von deutschen Torpedos getroffen worden.

Hauptsächlich ging es um die irische Kennzeichnung der Schiffe. Diese in der Hitze des Gefechts zu erkennen, mag oft schwierig gewesen sein, dennoch gab es rechtlich keine Entschuldigung für die zahlreichen 'Versehen'. Die irischen Proteste wurden in Berlin zwar entgegengenommen, man versprach auch Besserung, tatsächlich geschah jedoch nicht viel.

∝

Eine nicht minder schwere Belastung des deutsch-irischen Verhältnisses stellte die (ebenso 'versehentliche') deutsche Bombardierung irischen Territoriums dar. In der Luftschlacht um England, welche die deutsche Luftüberlegenheit für den Fall einer Invasion Englands herstellen sollte, nahmen deutsche Flugzeuge ihren Weg nach England oder Ulster vorzugsweise über die irische See oder entlang der irischen Ostküste. Dabei kam es offenbar nicht selten zu Verwechslungen, navigatorischen Fehlern, Orientierungsverlust insbesondere bei schlechtem Wetter und technischen Zwängen. Eine Rolle spielte dabei sicherlich, daß die irische Regierung den Briten hatte zugestehen müssen, die irischen Städte an der Ostküste zu verdunkeln, um den deutschen Flugzeugen nicht sozusagen eine beleuchtete Flugschneise zu bieten.

Der erste Bombenabwurf erfolgte am 26. August 1940 in der Grafschaft Waterford, und ihm folgten vor allem 1941 ein ganze Reihe weiterer Zwischenfälle mit zum Teil schweren Schäden und Verletzten, z. B. in Drogheda, Knockroe, dem Curragh, Enniskerry und in Terenure, einem Vorort von Dublin. Das schlimmste Bombardement ereignete sich am 30. Mai 1941 um Mitternacht über dem Dubliner Stadtteil Cabra (in der Nähe des Präsidentenpalais und der US Botschaft), wobei es 27 Tote und 120 Verletzte gab; 25 Häuser wurden total und 300 teilweise zerstört. Es gibt keine Anhaltspunkte dafür, daß Bomben absichtlich auf irisches Gebiet abgeworfen wurden; die Bombardements und zahlreichen anderen Verletzungen des irischen Luftraumes, gegen die Irland natürlich heftig protestierte, waren der Reichsregierung höchst peinlich, und man sagte stets Kompensation zu. Zwischen dem verstimmten Auswärtigen Amt und der Luftwaffe kam es zu einem beachtlichen bürokratischen Aufwand zur Aufklärung und Verhinderung solcher Vorfälle. Hitler, Göring und von Ribbentrop waren persönlich damit befaßt und gaben 'strikte' Anweisungen, es nicht noch einmal zu Zwischenfällen kommen zu lassen, jedoch ohne Erfolg. Erst mit dem Scheitern der Luftschlacht um Großbritannien und dem Abbruch der 'Operation Seeadler' zu Beginn des Rußlandfeldzugs 1941 hörten die Zwischenfälle auf. Daß ein Teil der irischen Bevölkerung die Dinge eher mit Geduld oder Fatalismus aufnahm und die Nationalisten davon ausgingen, britische Ablenkungstechniken (Laserstrahlen) seien für die Desorientierung der deutschen Flieger verantwortlich zu machen, erstaunt aus heutiger Sicht. Übrigens ging es auch um Nordirland, als britisches Territorium für die Luftwaffe ein 'legitimes' Ziel. Der Primas der katholischen Kirche, Kardinal MacRory, Erzbischof von Armagh und ein eher deutschfreundlicher Herr, bat Hempel mehrfach dringend dafür zu sorgen, daß das nordirische Armagh verschont werde. Die gleiche Bitte sprach Staatssekretär Joseph Walshe im Juni 1941 hinsichtlich des vorwiegend katholischen Derry aus, und 1944 brachte die irische Regierung ein ähnliches Anliegen hinsichtlich der elf irischen (meist religiösen) Einrichtungen in Rom vor.

ᑋ

Ein nicht minder irritierender Punkt war das Thema Spionage. Dabei ging es sowohl um laufende Wetter-beobachtung als auch um Informationen über die Aktivitäten der Alliierten in England und Nordirland; natürlich hatte die deutsche Botschaft die Aufgabe, einmal gewonnene Erkenntnisse weiterzugeben. Eine andere Sache aber war es, Spione in das Gastland einzuschleusen und zu unterstützen. Hier wurde die Grenze zwischen beiden

Aktivitäten verwischt, was zwei bekannte Fälle zeigen: Als im Zusammenhang mit der Schlacht um England der Gesandtschaft die Ein-schleusung von Agenten angekündigt worden war, wurde - an die Adresse der Spione gerichtet - vereinbart, in den Fenstern der Residenz des Gesandten bestimmte Blumenkästen als Signal dafür aufzustellen, daß die deutsche Invasion Englands beginne.

Im August 1942 erhielt Hempel von einem irischen Seemann, der in England gearbeitet hatte, die Nachricht, daß an einer bestimmten Stelle der englischen Südküste kanadische Einheiten zusammengezogen würden, und zwar mit dem Ziel einer Invasion bei Dieppe. In der Tat fand diese Operation am 19. August 1942 statt, wurde aber wohl aufgrund der Berichterstattung Hempels für die Alliierten zu einem Desaster.

Was die deutsche Spionage angeht, war die irische Seite stets hervorragend informiert, nicht zuletzt dadurch, daß die britischen und amerikanischen Geheimdienste in der Republik bestens funktionierten und mit den Iren zusammen-arbeiteten.

Die Deutschen machten in jenen Jahren zwei elementare Fehler: Sie setzten die anti-britischen Gefühle der Iren mit pro-deutschen gleich und sie überschätzten die Stärke und den Einfluß der IRA. Dafür waren sicherlich nicht nur Wunschdenken, sondern auch die 'Irlandexperten' in Berlin verantwortlich. Von deutscher Seite wurde auf ihren Rat hin immer wieder der Versuch unternommen, die vermeintliche Deutschfreundlichkeit und die unverwüstlichen Erwartungen nationalistischer Kreise zu nutzen, die mit Hilfe der Deutschen die Engländer aus Nordirland vertreiben wollten. De Valera hatte, wie oben berichtet, gerade davor gewarnt. Er wußte, daß die irische Neutralität nur durchzuhalten war, solange Irland nicht zur Basis anti-britischer Aktionen wurde. Im Laufe der Kriegsjahre geriet de Valera immer mehr unter Druck, vor allem von Seiten der Amerikanern. Ihr wenig diplomatisch agierender Botschafter David Gray, dessen Frau eine Verwandte von Eleonor Roosevelt war und der daher direkten Zugang zum Weißen Haus hatte, wurde nicht müde, deutsche Neutralitätsverletzungen aufzudecken und die sofortige Schließung der deutschen Gesandtschaft sowie die Aufgabe der irischen Neutralität zu fordern. Die britische Vertretung, die erst im September 1939 einen Leiter erhielt (England und Irland hatten sich jahrelang um seine Titulierung gestritten), tat das gleiche. Der neue 'UK Representative to Eire' (nicht 'Botschafter'), Sir John Maffey, war in seinen Methoden nur geschickter als sein amerikanischer Kollege. Hempel jedenfalls mußte fürchten, daß jede deutsche Spionage- und Wühlarbeit als Provokation gewertet und zu einem Eingreifen der Alliierten und dem Ende der irischen Neutralität führen konnte.

In der Tat befürchtete man nach dem Eintritt der USA in den Krieg nicht mehr eine deutsche, sondern eher eine alliierte Besetzung der Republik. Diese Möglichkeit wurde so konkret gesehen, daß die deutsche Gesandtschaft vorsorglich alle Geheimakten einschließlich die der NSDAP Ortsgruppe vernichtete. Bedrohlich schien es vor allem zu werden, als die USA begannen, im Rahmen des *Land Lease*-Abkommens ab 1941 in Nordirland Marine- und Luftstützpunkte aufzubauen. Rückblickend wird man sagen können, daß gerade die Möglichkeit des Ausweichens auf das britische Nordirland die irische Republik vor dem Schicksal einer alliierten Besetzung bewahrt hat. Die alliierten Vorbereitungen der Schlacht um Europa hätten ohne die nordirischen Basen wahrscheinlich zu einer Intervention geführt.

Eine deutsche Reaktion auf diese alliierten Okkupationsgefahr sei noch erwähnt: als man in Berlin dieser Bedrohung Irlands gewahr wurde, entstand dort der Gedanke, de Valera ein Hilfsangebot zu machen. Im Auswärtigen Amt war 1940 eine Sonderabteilung unter dem SS-Standartenführer Veesemeyer gebildet worden, die sich nur mit subversiven Aktionen befaßte. Irland war in diesem Kontext nur ein relativ kleiner Fisch. Die meisten größeren Aktionen betrafen Osteuropa. Veesemeyers Berater aus den Geheimdiensten vertraten die Auffassung, de Valera werde im Falle einer Besetzung durch die Alliierten sein Land mit allen Mitteln verteidigen.

Dr. Hellmut Clissmann (vor dem Krieg Vertreter des DAAD in Dublin), der im Rang eines Unteroffiziers zunächst bei der Canaris'schen Abwehr tätig, dann zu Veesemeyers

Büro abgeordnet worden war, fuhr im Januar 1942 in dessen Auftrag nach Madrid. Dort konsultierte er den als rechtslastig bekannten irischen Botschafter Leopold Kerney, ein vermeintlicher Freund de Valeras. Kerney vertrat die Meinung, de Valera werde in der Tat sich im Ernstfall zur Wehr setzen, die Deutschen zu Hilfe rufen und mit Deutschland eine gemeinsame Front bilden. Sobald Irland angegriffen werde, schließe sich die bestehende Kluft zwischen de Valera und der IRA.

CR

Im Februar 1942 wurde Hempel beauftragt, bei de Valera diesbezüglich zu sondieren, insbesondere zu fragen, ob er gegebenenfalls Waffen annähme. De Valera ging zur Enttäuschung Hempels mit keinem einzigen Wort auf Hempels Fragen ein, sondern wechselte das Thema. In Berlin glaubte man jedoch den 'Irland-Experten' mehr als Hempel. Man meinte, dort auf eine solche Möglichkeit oder Chance vorbereitet sein zu müssen. Nach mehreren Gesprächen mit Reichsaußenminister von Ribbentrop, der auch Hitler unterrichtete, beschloß man, nach einem Plan des SS-Standartenführers Schellenberg, eine Spezialtruppe von etwa 120 ausgesuchten SS-Leuten aufzustellen und sich auf den Eventualfall eines irischen Hilfeersuchens vorzubereiten. Die Hempelsche Berichterstattung wirkte aber doch ernüchternd, und letztlich sollte sich der federführende Veesemeyer darauf beschränken, zehn bis zwölf Mann mit dem Ziel zu beschäftigen, *"die vorhandenen irischen Widerstandskräfte zu mobilisieren, zu unterstützen und einen einwandfrei arbeitenden Nachrichtenapparat zu schaffen"*. An diesen haperte es aber.

CR

Die Aktivitäten der deutschen Spionage in Irland ähnelten im großen und ganzen einer schlechten Komödie: Da war der Fall Goertz, der für die Gesandtschaft zu einem Dauerproblem werden sollte. Der Hauptmann der Abwehr Dr.

Hermann Goertz (Deckname 'Doktor') war am 6. Mai 1940 mit dem Fallschirm in County Meath gelandet. Sein Ziel war allerdings Laragh im County Wicklow gewesen, wo er schließlich nach einem langen Fußmarsch bei der Frau von Francis Stuart, Iseult Stuart, auch Obdach fand. Iseult wurde später deshalb verhaftet, aber letztlich freigesprochen. Anders erging es Goertzens irischem V-Mann namens Held in Dalkey. Dieser wurde infolge seiner leicht zu entdeckenden Funkarbeit gefaßt und zu 5 Jahren Gefängnis verurteilt. Bei Held war der sogenannte 'Plan Kathleen' gefunden worden, der eine deutsche Landung in Derry mit Unterstützung der IRA vorsah. Die herrschende Meinung geht davon aus, daß dies eine Idee der IRA, kein deutscher Plan war. Goertz gelang es, sich bis Dezember 1941 u.a. auch bei den Schwestern Farrell in Dun Laoghaire versteckt zu halten. Er hatte zwar gelegentlich Funkkontakt mit deutschen Stellen, man fragt sich aber, was er wohl zu berichten hatte, sein Auftrag lautete nämlich: *"Sabotageakte gegen Großbritannien vorzubereiten, eventuell durchzuführen in Zusammenarbeit mit der IRA, ohne jedoch die irische Regierung zu belasten."* Wie oben dargelegt, war gerade das die Quadratur des Kreises. Goertzens Aktivitäten erwiesen sich bald als fruchtlos, für ihn wie auch für die Deutschen in Irland eher peinlich. Er war frustriert und fühlte sich auch finanziell im Stich gelassen (Hempel berichtete von ernsthaften Depressionen). Zweimal versuchte Goertz vergeblich, mit einem Motorboot zu entkommen. Selbst Veesemeyer und der Unterstaatssekretär im Auswärtigen Amt Woermann bezeichneten ihn als 'Belastung', nachdem er Ende 1941 festgegommen und interniert worden war.

Ein weiterer Agent war der sechzigjährige ehemalige Preisboxer Weber-Drohl, der im März 1940 als Geldkurier für die IRA auftauchte. Auch er wurde schnell gefaßt und wegen seines schlechten Gesundheitszustandes ebenfalls (nur) interniert.

In diese Reihe gehören auch die beiden Südafrikaner Gartner, Tributh und der Inder Obed, die im Juli 1940 in deutschem Auftrag an der irischen Südküste abgesetzt wurden. Einer Anekdote zufolge sprach einer von ihnen einen irischen Busfahrer in perfektem Gälisch an und fragte nach dem Namen der nächsten Ortschaft. Die guten Gälischkenntnisse machten unseren Helden so suspekt, daß das Dreigespann umgehend verhaftet wurde. Hinzu kam peinlicherweise noch, daß alle drei nur irische Pfundnoten mit fortlaufenden Seriennummern besaßen.

Walter Simon alias Karl Anderson, Willy Preetz alias Paddy Mitchell ebenso wie Günter Schulz alias Hans Marschner, Van Loon und Werner B. Umland, alle im Spionageauftrag 1940/41 von U-Booten angelandet oder mit dem Fallschirm abgesprungen, wurden ebenso nach kurzer Zeit gefaßt.

ଓଃ

Gewichtiger als all diese schlecht vorbereiteten Spionageversuche erscheinen die Pläne, im Ausland lebende IRA Männer nach Irland zurückzuschleusen, den linken mit dem rechten Flügel der Bewegung auszusöhnen und damit die Bewegung für gemeinsame Aktionen gegen England zu stärken. Im August 1940 wurde zunächst der (rechte) IRA Führer Séan Russell mit einem deutschen U-Boot aus den USA geholt und mit dem (linken) Frank Ryan zusammengebracht. Beide machten sich zusammen auf nach Irland. Während der U-Bootfahrt von Deutschland nach Irland (100 Meilen vor Galway) verstarb Russell in den Armen Ryans an einem durchgebrochenen Magengeschwür. Ryan kehrte nach Deutschland zurück, und alle Hoffnung konzentrierte sich jetzt auf ihn. Er hatte im spanischen Bürgerkrieg auf republikanischer Seite gekämpft, war vom Franco-Regime zum Tode verurteilt, dann aber auf Drängen de Valeras zu lebenslänglicher Haft begnadigt und schließlich auf deutsche Intervention hin freigelassen worden. In Berlin angekommen, galt er von Anfang an als der "wichtigste Ire" und wurde von Veesemeyer persönlich betreut. Kurz vor einem zweiten 'Einsatz-Versuch' in Irland erlitt er am 13. Januar 1943 einen Schlaganfall, lag zunächst in der Berliner Charité und starb dann in einem Sanatorium bei Dresden an Lungenentzündung.

1942 scheiterte noch ein weiterer deutscher Anlauf. Agenten sollten mit Wasserflugzeugen abgesetzt werden, um die IRA mit Geld und Funkgeräten zu versorgen. Es gab mehrere Besprechungen mit von Ribbentrop auf Schloß Fuschl, ebenso wie mit Veesemeyer in Zagreb. Von Ribbentrop war eher skeptisch und bremste. Alles scheiterte letztlich daran, daß die Marine es ablehnte, Wasserflugzeuge zur Verfügung zu stellen.

Für Ende 1942 verzeichnen die Akten noch ein Ersuchen der IRA um Waffen, Geld und Ausbildung. Als endlich im Dezember 1943 nahe Kilkee in der Grafschaft Limerick zwei Iren - angeblich im Auftrag der deutschen Marine - mit Funkgeräten und Geld per Fallschirm absprangen, wurden sie umgehend verhaftet.

In die Kategorie 'Sandkastenspiele' gehören auch zwei militärische Planungen. Im Rahmen der Schlacht um England veranlaßte General Leonhard Kaupisch, der Kommandeur des 4. und 7. Armeecorps in Frankreich, die Ausarbeitung eines Invasionsplans gegen Irland. Es erscheint wahrscheinlich, daß dies entweder als reine militärische Übung oder als Spielmaterial zur Irreführung des Gegners geschah.

Bestanden hat auch ein Operationsplan 'Grün', wonach - im Fall einer Invasion Englands - zum Flankenschutz in Irland ein Brückenkopf *Gorey, Mount Leinster, Thomastown, Clonmel, Dungarvan* gebildet werden sollte. Die Ernsthaftigkeit dieser Idee darf rückblickend auch bezweifelt werden.

ଔ

Zu guter Letzt soll der Versuch nicht unerwähnt bleiben, aus britischen Kriegsgefangenen irischer Abstammung eine 'Irische Brigade' zu bilden. Man hatte offenbar aus Roger Casements gescheitertem Unternehmen gleicher Art von 1916/17 nicht das Geringste gelernt. In der Tat wurden die irischen Briten in einem gesonderten Lager in Friesack (Brandenburg) zusammengefaßt; die Bemühungen, die Soldaten 'umzudrehen', mißlangen jedoch völlig.

Ein weiteres Kreuz, das die Gesandtschaft zu tragen hatte und das die deutsch-irischen Beziehungen belastete, waren die zahlreichen in Irland internierten Deutschen. Irland hatte bis zum Zusammenbruch des Dritten Reiches uneingeschränkte diplomatische Beziehungen mit Berlin, dadurch konnten sich Deutsche und Iren im jeweiligen Land unbehindert aufhalten. Es war jedoch völlig korrekt, Militärpersonal, welches das Territorium des anderen Staates unerlaubt betrat, festzunehmen und zu internieren. Im Laufe des Krieges gelangten mehr als 250 deutsche Personen in irische Internierung in einem Lager im Curragh in der Grafschaft Kildare. Die meisten von ihnen waren, neben den oben aufgeführten Agenten, schiffsbrüchige Matrosen und abgesprungene oder notgelandete Flieger.

Das erste Flugzeug war schon am 20. August 1940 am Mount Brandon auf der Dingle Halbinsel abgestürzt. Unter den geretteten Fliegern befand sich auch Oberleutnant Kurt Mollenhauer, der von da an bis 1944 Lagerältester im *Curragh Camp* war. Es folgten Dutzende weiterer Abstürze und Notlandungen.

Die Zahl der Internierten stieg Anfang 1944 stark an. Am 29. Dezember 1943 rettete die Besatzung des irischen Frachters *Kerlogue* in einer einmalig selbstlosen und heldenhaften Aktion 168 deutsche schiffbrüchige Matrosen, deren drei Schiffe, ein Zerstörer und zwei MTBs, zwischen Brest und St. Nazaire versenkt worden waren. Die irische *Kerlogue* (335 Tonnen) wurde durch die Aufnahme der Deutschen gefährlich überlastet. Ihr Kapitän, Donoghue, bewies aber auch dadurch Mut, daß er den Instruktionen zuwider kein 'Navicert' der Briten im britischen Fishguard einholte und die Aufforderung der Engländer ignorierte, die Deutschen an England auszuliefern. Der Protest Sir John Maffeys, des britischen 'Botschafters' in Dublin, kam zu spät. Im März 1945 gesellten sich zu diesen Matrosen weitere 48 Deutsche eines U-Boots, das vor der Küste Corks sank.

Alle Internierten wurden gut und freundlich behandelt, hatten häufigen Ausgang, konnten im benachbarten

Newbridge Tennis spielen, die örtlichen Pubs und Cafés in Dublin besuchen. Viele pflegten Freundschaften mit irischen Mädchen, und fünf von ihnen heirateten nach dem Krieg Irinnen. Natürlich konnte die Versorgungslage im Lager nicht besser sein als die der irischen Bevölkerung selbst, und diese war aufgrund des faktischen Embargos eher schlecht. Auch machten Heimweh, die Monotonie des Lagerlebens, die Ungewißheit über den Kriegsverlauf und die unvermeidbaren Reibereien unter den Insassen vielen zu schaffen. Frustration, Ungeduld und Langeweile waren daher Dauererscheinungen. Es kam zu Fluchtversuchen, zu Beschwerden und zu Problemen der Disziplin.

Die Gesandtschaft versuchte, so gut wie möglich zu vermitteln und bei den irischen Behörden das Los der Internierten zu erleichtern. Es gelang sogar durchzusetzen, daß einige von ihnen an der Universität studieren und zeitweise in Dublin wohnen durften.

Am Ende des Krieges waren es 266 deutsche Militärpersonen, die repatriiert werden sollten; davon waren die Agenten nicht betroffen. Keiner wurde gezwungen, in die Sowjetisch Besetzte Zone (SBZ) zu gehen. Nur 138 meldeten sich freiwillig zur Rückkehr, 50 baten bleiben zu dürfen. Dem wurde nicht entsprochen und bis auf ganz wenige, die sich mit Irinnen liiert hatten, verließen letztlich alle die Grüne Insel.

Der Historiker Dwyer schildert, wie die Internierten am 13. August 1945 mit dem britischen Schiff HMS *St Andrews* Irland verließen. Die britische Besatzung des Dampfers traute ihren Augen nicht: Da marschierte eine Kolonne wohl gekleideter und gut genährter Herren, fließend Englisch sprechend, mit Tennisschlägern und Angeln unter dem Arm, an Bord. Der Internierte Voigt soll einen Briten sagen gehört haben: *"Was, das sollen deutsche Soldaten sein? Das sind doch Touristen!"*

Die sieben internierten Agenten verblieben zunächst in Irland. Ihnen wurde im September 1946 formell Asyl gewährt. Schultz und Van Loon heirateten Irinnen und konnten auf Dauer in Irland bleiben. Als im April 1947 in Deutschland die Kriegsverbrecherprozesse begannen, verlangten die Alliierten die Auslieferung dieses Personenkreises.

Goertz, der bereits vor dem Krieg als Spion in britischer Haft war, geriet in Panik. Er bemühte sich vergeblich, nach Südamerika zu gelangen. Im Aliens Registration Office (Dublin Castle) nahm er sich kurz vor der Auslieferung durch Gift das Leben. Er hatte nach dem Krieg unermüdlich an der Aktion *Save the German Children*, über die noch berichtet wird, mitgearbeitet.

CR

Erstaunlicherweise kam es auch nach dem Ende des Krieges noch zu einem Zwischenfall mit deutschen Soldaten. Mitte Januar 1946 konnte eine Gruppe deutscher Kriegsgefangener - von den Franzosen in St. Nazaire als Minensucher eingesetzt - sich bei Nacht und Nebel eines Minensuchboots bemächtigen und nach Irland entkommen. Sie landeten in Kinsale in der Grafschaft Cork, wurden dort aufs freundlichste empfangen und von den Bürgern des charmanten Hafenstädtchens gut betreut . Doch schon nach einigen Tagen war das Glück zu Ende: auf englischen und französischen Druck hin sah sich die irische Regierung gezwungen, die Gruppe nebst Minensuchboot auszuliefern.

CR

Ein ganz besonderes Sorgenkind war während der Kriegsjahre die technische Kommunikation mit Berlin. Die Vertretung besaß einen geheimen Sender, mit dem zunächst direkt, dann ab Mitte 1941 über die deutsche Gesandtschaft Bern gearbeitet wurde. Dieser Sender war vom irischen Geheimdienst und von den Alliierten bereits im Januar 1940 geortet worden. Von da an ließ der britische Geheimdienst nicht locker, die irische Regierung auf diese „Irregularität" hinzuweisen. Der Sender wurde zum ständigen Stein des Anstoßes. Die deutsche Seite war auf dieses Kommunikationsmittel angewiesen, da der einzig mögliche Kurierweg über London wohl zurecht als nicht sicher galt. Die reguläre telegraphische Verbindung lief ebenfalls über London, war aber langsam und sicherheitsmäßig unbrauchbar.

Die irische Regierung sah sich unter alliiertem Druck gezwungen, Hempel immer wieder auf den Sender anzusprechen. Das geschah lange Zeit nur als Pflichtübung; Hempel sagte Staatssekretär Joseph Walshe schon im April 1941 zu, den Sender normalerweise nicht, sondern nur in 'ganz dringenden Fällen' zu benutzen. Da dieses Kriterium kaum überprüfbar war, blieb alles einige Zeit in der Schwebe. Im August 1941 sprach de Valera Hempel auf die Angelegenheit an, und Hempel wiederholte seine Zusage. Die Beweise der alliierten Geheimdienste für die tatsächliche deutsche Funkpraxis und die Demarchen der Amerikaner und Briten wurden im Laufe des Jahres 1942 so massiv, daß der sonst deutschfreundliche Walshe Hempel im Oktober 1942 ernsthaft verwarnte und Maßnahmen androhte. Es dauerte aber noch bis zum Dezember 1943, bis de Valera ultimativ die Ablieferung des Senders verlangte. Hempel konnte sich der Forderung nicht mehr entziehen. Schweren Herzens funkte er am 17. Dezember 1943 einen letzten Bericht nach Berlin. Er enthielt die Weihnachtsbotschaft de Valeras an das irische Volk. Danach trat Funkstille ein. Der Sender wurde kurz vor Weihnachten 1943 von Hempel und Walshe gemeinsam geradezu feierlich in einem Banksafe deponiert, zu dem beide je einen von zwei verschiedenen Schlüsseln hatten.

Die Unmöglichkeit, von Berlin betreut zu werden, führte spätestens Anfang 1944 zu allgemeinen Schwierigkeiten, vor allem in der Geldversorgung. Die Gesandtschaft war buchstäblich zahlungsunfähig. Hempel versuchte, Forderungen deutscher Firmen gegen irische Schuldner einzutreiben und ging deswegen sogar vor Gericht, jedoch ohne Erfolg. Auf Veranlassung de Valeras erhielt die Gesandtschaft schließlich ein Darlehen. Hempel und de Valera kamen auf die Idee, ein deutsch-irisches Kriegsschädenabkommen abzuschließen, das die Situation rettete. Es konnte am 1. Februar 1945 in Kraft treten. Danach war die irische Regierung berechtigt, Forderungen Deutscher gegen Iren einzuziehen und auf ein Sonderkonto einzuzahlen, aus dem die Unkosten der deutschen Gesandtschaft, der Unterhalt der deutschen Internierten und die Regulierung der Bombenschäden bestritten wurde. Die Bombenschäden wurden übrigens ganz bewußt niedrig auf nur £40.000 veranschlagt. Später, im Jahre 1953, sollten die tatsächlichen Kosten fast mit einer halben Million Pfund beziffert werden.

CR

Eine letzte, unvergessene Episode ist vom Mai 1945 zu berichten. Hitler hatte sich am 30. April 1945 das Leben genommen. Mit seiner Person war, formal gesehen, ein Staatsoberhaupt gestorben. Dem internationalen Brauch entsprechend legte die Gesandtschaft ein Kondolenzbuch auf, in das man sich eintragen konnte. Am 2. Mai 1945 begaben sich Taoiseach (Ministerpräsident) Eamon de Valera, der Staatssekretär im Außenamt, Joseph Walshe und der Sekretär des Staatspräsidenten Douglas Hyde, Michael McDunphy, zu einem Kondolenzbesuch in die Residenz (nicht die Kanzlei) des Gesandten Hempel. Damit sollte auch der Respekt vor der Person Hempels zum Ausdruck gebracht werden. Die formelle Geste entsprach dem internationalen Protokoll, führte aber zu einem Aufschrei in der britischen und amerikanischen Presse und ist bis zum heutigen Tage eine der umstrittensten Aktionen de Valeras.

CR

Die ersten Monate des Jahres 1945 waren eine Zeit großer Ungewißheit darüber, ob Irland dem Beispiel so vieler Staaten folgen würde, die noch kurz vor Kriegsende ihren neutralen Status aufgaben und dem Reich den Krieg erklärten, um nach dem Kriege auf der richtigen Seite, nämlich derjenigen der Siegermächte, zu sein. Irland tat nichts desgleichen.

Bereits Monate vor der deutschen Kapitulation verlangte der amerikanische Botschafter David Gray die Schließung der deutschen Gesandtschaft, die Herausgabe ihrer Registratur und der Archive, was de Valera ablehnte. Sir John Maffey war auch dagegen, Außenminister Eden hielt es für überflüssig, da alles Wichtige ohnehin vernichtet sei.

Churchill aber entschied, daß Gray mit seiner Forderung zu unterstützen sei.

Am 10. Mai 1945 ließ es sich nicht mehr länger vermeiden: Die Schlüssel der Gesandtschaft mußten an Botschafter Gray übergeben werden. Auf einer Auktion in Belfast erzielte der Verkauf der gesamten beweglichen Gegenstände der Gesandtschaft £1760. Das Kanzleigebäude wurde Großbritannien zugesprochen und später veräussert.

Die Angehörigen der ehemaligen deutschen Vertretung zogen sich ins Privatleben zurück oder warteten auf ihre Repatriierung. De Valera gewährte dem Gesandten Hempel, den er über all die Jahre schätzen gelernt hatte, formell Asyl. Daß er den Gesandten, der mit dem Ende der Reichsregierung in niemandes Sold mehr stand, auch finanziell unterstützt hat, wurde behauptet, ist aber nicht bewiesen. Sicher ist, daß Familie Hempel im Dubliner Stadtteil Monkstown eher schlecht als recht überleben mußte; Frau Hempel erwies sich glücklicherweise als gute Bäckerin und handelte mit Backwaren. Hempel gelang es erst 1949, übrigens mit Hilfe seines ehemaligen britischen Kollegen Sir John Maffey, in die Bundesrepublik zurückzukehren, und zwar ins Auswärtige Amt in Bonn auf den Posten, den er vor 1937 innehatte. Es blieben ihm nur noch wenige Jahre aktiven Dienstes, dann trat er in den Ruhestand. Er starb 85-jährig am 12. November 1972 in Freiburg.

8. Nachkriegsjahre

Die Jahre unmittelbar nach dem 2. Weltkrieg standen im Zeichen irischer Großherzigkeit. Wie immer wieder in der Geschichte ergriffen die Iren die Partei der *underdogs*, dieses Mal der geschlagenen Deutschen. Neben Geld- und Sachspenden war es die freiwillige Mitarbeit in internationalen Hilfsorganisationen, z.B. von irischen Krankenschwestern und Ärzten in UN Organisationen, die zu erwähnen ist. Neben dem Roten Kreuz waren vor allem die katholischen Verbände aktiv. Die alten Kontakte zwischen den Kirchen beider Länder lebten wieder auf und erwiesen sich als wertvoll.

CR

Unvergeßlich bleiben nicht nur die umfangreichen Hilfslieferungen (Butter, Speck, Zucker) sondern auch die Aktion *Save the German Children,* die von einer Gesellschaft getragen wurde, welche am 16. Oktober 1945 Dr. Kathleen Murphy mit anderen zusammen gegründet hatte. Sie versuchte, über das Rote Kreuz aus dem zerstörten Deutschland vor allem Waisenkinder nach Irland zu bringen. Das war jedoch nicht einfach: Zum einen fehlte es in Deutschland an der erforderlichen Infrastruktur, zum anderen gab es Widerstände sowohl im eigenen Land als auch bei den alliierten Behörden in den Besatzungszonen. Die Mitglieder der Gesellschaft ließen aber nicht locker. Schließlich gelang es, bis zum Oktober 1946 190 deutsche Kinder nach Irland zu bringen. 134 konnten sofort in irischen Familien untergebracht werden, und im November kamen weitere 126 hinzu. Alle Transporte wurden vom Irischen Roten Kreuz durchgeführt. Im April 1947 stieg die Zahl auf 418, bis 1948 auf 518 Kinder an. Insgesamt erbrachten die Sammlungen für die Aktion 1,3 Millionen DM.

Die Kinder waren zunächst für drei Jahre zugewiesen. Viele Familien wollten die Kinder jedoch behalten, und es kam zu emotional schwierigen Situationen. Schließlich konnten etwa 50 Kinder auf Dauer bei ihren irischen Pflegeeltern bleiben.

Ein Zeichen der Dankbarkeit steht im Dubliner St. Stephen's Green Park. Hier erinnert der *Nornenbrunnen*, eine große Bronzeskulptur des Bildhauers Josef Wackerle, an die Aktion. Bundespräsident Theodor Heuß hat das Denkmal aufstellen lassen, um dankend an die Hilfe des irischen Volkes zu erinnern.

Die Aktion *Save the German Children* war es auch, die zur Gründung einer deutschen Schule in Dublin führte. Aus den bescheidenen Anfängen einer Sonntagsschule entwickelte sich *St. Kilian's - Deutsche Schule* zu einer der angesehensten pädagogischen Anstalten Dublins. Sie ist heute eine Gesamtschule mit Schwerpunkt 'Deutsche Sprache', die über die Jahre Hunderte von deutschen wie irischen Schülern zum irischen Sekundarschulabschluß geführt hat.

❧

Die amtlichen Beziehungen ließen noch lange auf sich warten. Nach ihrer Gründung besaß die Bundesrepublik keineswegs sofort die volle Souveränität und damit das Recht, diplomatische Beziehungen mit anderen Staaten zu unterhalten. Irland war einer der ersten Staaten, der sich um offizielle Verbindungen bemühte. Am 17. Januar 1951 fand diesbezüglich in Bonn das erste Gespräch zwischen dem irischen Sonderbotschafter John A.Belton und Staatsrat Haas vom Büro Adenauer statt. Für März 1951 stellte Haas die Einrichtung eines Generalkonsulats in Dublin in Aussicht. Irland erklärte sich mit dem Austausch von Konsulaten für die Zeit einverstanden, in der das Besatzungsstatut diplomatische Beziehungen noch ausschloß. Belton legte Wert darauf zu vermeiden, bei den Alliierten Hochkommissaren der Besatzungsmächte um Agrément nachsuchen und ein Beglaubigungsscheiben überreichen zu müssen.

Am 18. Januar 1951 war die Bewilligung von Personalstellen auf der Tagesordnung des Deutschen Bundestags. Zum Verdruß der Bundesregierung wurde für ein Generalkonsulat in Dublin nicht wie beantragt die 1. sondern nur die 2. Klasse bewilligt, irgend etwas war bei der Erläuterung des Antrags schief gelaufen. Man gab sich damit nicht zufrieden, zumal ein bestimmter hochrangiger Kandidat für den Posten hinter den Kulissen schon wartete. Die Sache wurde am 3. Februar desselben Jahres erneut in den Bundestag gebracht mit der Begründung, weltweit würde die deutsche Vertretung in Dublin als einzige nicht ihren Vorkriegsstatus zurückerhalten, und die Abgeordneten gaben schließlich nach.

Eine Rolle dabei spielte sicherlich der Kandidat für den Dubliner Posten. Am 27. Januar 1951 hatte der Bonner General-Anzeiger völlig regelwidrig und verfrüht gemeldet, dem ehemaligen Pressesprecher des nordrheinwestfälischen Ministerpräsidenten Arnold und jetzigen Direktor des Bundesrats, Dr. Dr. Katzenberger, sei die Stelle zugedacht.

Katzenberger war in der Weimarer Zeit unter anderem Generalsekretär der Zentrumspartei gewesen und war dann in den Auswärtigen Dienst eingetreten. Dies war aber nur von kurzer Dauer, nach 1933 wurde er als 'politisch unzuverlässig' entlassen. Am 11. April 1951 sprach Belton etwas ungeduldig beim Chef des Protokolls im Kanzleramt, Schwarzmann, vor, um sich nach dem Termin für die Eröffnung der Dubliner Vertretung zu erkundigen. Er dachte wohl (wegen der Gegenseitigkeit) an seine eigene Lage; denn am 11. Juni 1951 sollte er Bundespräsident Heuß sein Beglaubigungsschreiben übergeben. Schwarzmann erklärte die Verzögerung damit, daß eine Revision des Besatzungsstatutes zu erwarten sei, die es der Bundesregierung ermögliche, eigene diplomatische Vertretungen zu unterhalten. Katzenberger solle als Gesandter, nicht als Generalkonsul, nach Dublin geschickt werden. So kam es denn auch. Im Juni 1951 trafen die ersten Mitarbeiter der neuen deutschen Vertretung in Dublin ein. Sie wohnten zunächst im Parkside Hotel in der North Circular Road. Mit Hilfe des irischen Protokollchefs McDonald, des schweizerischen Botschafters und des

Rechtsanwalts Arthur Cox war das Wesentlichste für die Eröffnung einer Gesandt-schaft bald arrangiert. Katzenberger selbst traf am 20. Juni 1951 ein und wohnte anfangs im Shelbourne Hotel. Am 12. Juli 1951 überreichte er dem irischen Staatspräsidenten O'Kelly sein Beglaubigungsschreiben. In Bonn trat an die Stelle von John Belton 1955 Dr. Thomas Joseph (Tom) Kiernan, der bereits 1939 diese Funktion hatte übernehmen sollen - sozusagen mit sechzehnjähriger Verzögerung. Katzenberger trat 1956, Kiernan 1957 in den Ruhestand.

ଔ

Im August 1952 besuchte Séan Lemass als Tanaiste, und somit als erster irischer Minister, die Bundesrepublik. Was vom Krieg im deutsch-irischen Zusammenhang übrig geblieben war, wurde aufgearbeitet. Unter Bezugnahme auf jenes Abkommen vom 2. Februar 1945 wurden alle gegenseitigen Ansprüche aufgerechnet. Der Nettoüberschuß der von irischen Stellen eingetriebenen Gelder betrug £51.646, die deutsche Entschädigungsverpflichtung £446.820. Bonn säumte nicht, den Saldo von £395.173 zu zahlen. Ein ganz neues Kapitel freundschaftlicher Beziehungen zwischen den Regierungen und der Bevölkerung Deutschlands und Irlands begann.

ଔ

Nur zögerlich kamen die ersten Deutschen, um die mysteriöse 'Grüne Insel' zu entdecken. Erst der immer frostiger werdende kalte Krieg im Zentrum Deutschlands, vor allem aber die Ereignisse in Budapest, in Prag und dann der Bau der Berliner Mauer, lenkten die Blicke zahlreicher Deutscher hin auf die entfernte Peripherie Europas, nach Irland. Vielleicht würden die Sowjets die kleine Bundesrepublik doch noch vereinnahmen? War es da nicht naheliegend, sich ein Refugium in Irland zu sichern? So kam es nach 1956 und erneut 1961 in Irland zu den ersten Investitionen deutscher Landwirte und mittelständischer Unternehmer und zum Kauf von Farmen, Herrenhäusern und

175

Cottages, an denen der irische Immobilienmarkt keinen Mangel hatte.

Ganz wenige hatten schon vorher, in den ersten Nachkriegsjahren, dem Kontinent den Rücken gekehrt und in Irland dauerhaft Zuflucht gefunden. Der erste war Prinz Ernst Heinrich von Sachsen, der jüngste von drei Söhnen des ehemaligen sächsischen Königs Friedrich August III., der bereits Anfang 1947 in Irland eintraf. Wie es ihm und seiner Familie noch vor der Gründung der Bundesrepublik gelang, sich in Irland anzusiedeln, ist erwähnenswert. Prinz Ernst Heinrich, ein Diplomlandwirt, dem die Verwaltung des Besitzes der Wettiner oblag, hatte seinen Wohnsitz, die Moritzburg bei Dresden, unter abenteuerlichen Umständen mit wenig Habe erst verlassen, als die Russen schon Görlitz erobert hatten. Mit seiner jungen (zweiten) Frau und drei Söhnen fand er Obdach bei seiner Schwester, der Fürstin von Hohenzollern-Sigmaringen. Sein älterer Bruder Christian, der Chef des Hauses Wettin, Markgraf von Meißen, hatte beim Herzog von Württemberg Unterschlupf gefunden. Nach der Besetzung Sigmaringens durch die Franzosen entstand sehr bald Kontakt mit adligen französischen Offizieren. Diese bekamen Wind von einer der ganz wenigen Kostbarkeiten, die Prinz Ernst Heinrich in seinem Fluchtgepäck hatte mitnehmen können, nämlich die Krone Ludwig IX. des Heiligen, des berühmten französischen Königs des 13. Jahrhunderts (1226-70). Sie war in altem Wettiner Besitz und überstand den Luftangriff auf Dresden 1945 in einem Safe, der nach dem Bombardement hoch oben in einer Wand der Ruine des Stadtschlosses hing. Mit Hilfe der Feuerwehr hatte Prinz Ernst sie noch kurz vor seiner Flucht retten können.

Die französische Regierung in Paris zögerte nicht lange und nahm mit den beiden Sachsenprinzen Verhandlungen auf mit dem Ziel, der Krone habhaft zu werden. Die Franzosen erklärten sich im Tausch für die Krone bereit, Prinz Ernst, der im Westen keinen Besitz hatte, bei der Existenzgründung behilflich zu sein. Er habe nur zu sagen, was er zu tun beabsichtige. In seinem Bedürfnis, das zerstörte und 1946 hoffnungslos erscheinende Deutschland zu verlassen, beschloß Prinz Ernst Heinrich, sich in Irland als

Landwirt niederzulassen. Wieso er diese Wahl traf, bleibt sein Geheimnis. Beeinflußt hatte ihn sicher die Tatsache, daß sein langjähriger und von ihm hochverehrter Erzieher ein Ire war, der sich Baron O'Byrne nannte.

Paris nahm mit Dublin Verhandlungen auf und veranlaßte, daß Prinz Ernst Heinrich eine irische Aufenthalts- und Ankaufserlaubnis erhielt. Mit Hilfe der französischen Entschädigungssumme übernahm die Familie daraufhin 1947 ein landwirtschaftliches Anwesen in der irischen Grafschaft Westmeath, das sie unter großem persönlichen Einsatz zu einer blühenden Vieh- und Milchwirtschaft ausbaute. Die Krone selbst wurde von den beiden Wettiner Prinzen in einer feierlichen Zeremonie in der Sainte Chapelle in Paris übergeben und befindet sich jetzt im Louvre. Prinz Ernst Heinrich starb in Westmeath 74-jährig im Jahre 1971.

ଔ

Die intensivere Begegnung unserer beiden Völker nach dem 2. Weltkrieg verdanken wir Heinrich Böll, der mit seinem *Irischen Tagebuch*, welches 1957 erschien, sofort und bis heute das Interesse weiter Kreise in Deutschland wach rief. Sein Buch war ein Bestseller und löste eine Reisewelle aus, die zu einem festen Stamm deutscher Irlandliebhaber geführt hat. Der rasante technische Fortschritt der Kommunikationsmittel trug das Seine dazu bei.

Über die Böllsche Schilderung der so romantischen Rückständigkeit Irlands in den fünfziger Jahren war das offizielle Irland zunächst keineswegs glücklich. Erst die Irlandbegeisterung, die Bölls Tagebuch auslöste, versöhnte 'das Irland auf dem Weg zu einer modernen Gesellschaft'. Böll selbst hat in seinem Essay *Dreizehn Jahre später* zugegeben, daß sich in Irland schon in den sechziger Jahren viel verändert hatte

"als hätten wir in den Jahren 1954 und 1955 Irland in jenem historischen Augenblick erwischt, wo es gerade anfing, eineinhalb Jahrhunderte zu überspringen und sich von fünf weiteren einholen zu lassen."

Er ließ es offen, ob er noch immer glaubte, was er 1957 gesagt hatte, nämlich, *"daß die Iren näher am Himmel wohnen als die übrigen Europäer"*.

In seinem Cottage auf der westirischen Insel Achill empfand er das wohl so.

Bibliography / Literaturverzeichnis

Baumgarten, Rolf   Bibliography of Irish Linguistics and Literature 1942-71
Dublin, Institute for Advanced Studies 1986

Bell, Bowyer J.   The Secret Army: A History of the IRA 1915-1970
London, Sphere Books 1972

Bewley, Charles   Memoirs of a Wild Goose
Dublin, Lilliput Press 1989

Bewley, Charles   Hermann Göring and the Third Reich
New York, Devin-Adair 1962

Carroll, Joseph T.   Ireland in the War Years
London, David & Charles 1975

Carter, Carole J.   Shamrock and Swastika: German Espionage in Ireland in World War II
Palo Alto, Pacific Books 1977

Cole, J.A.   Lord Haw-Haw
London, Faber and Faber 1987

Coogan, Tim Pat   Ireland Since the Rising
London, Pall Mall Press 1966

Coogan, Tim Pat   The IRA
London, Fontana 1966

Cronin, Séan

Frank Ryan - The Search
for the Republic
Dublin, Repsol Publishing 1980

Dickel, Horst

Die deutsche Außenpolitik und die
irische Frage von 1932 bis 1944
Wiesbaden, Steiner Verlag 1983

Doerries, Reinhard

Die Mission Sir Roger Casements
im Deutschen Reich 1914-16
Historische Zeitschrift 222, 1976

Duggan, John P.

Herr Hempel at the German
Legation in Dublin 1937-45
PhD Dissertation Trinity
College Dublin 1980

Duggan, John P.

Neutral Ireland and the Third Reich
Dublin, Gill & Macmillan 1985

Dwyer, Ryle T.

De Valera - The Man and the
Myths
Dublin, Poolbeg 1992

Dwyer, Ryle T.

Guests of State - The Story of
Allied and Axis Servicemen
Interned in Ireland During
World War II
Dingle, Brandon 1994

Elborn, Geoffrey

Francis Stuart - A Life
Dublin, Raven Arts Press 1990

Fisk, Robert

In Time of War: Ireland,
Ulster and the Price of
Neutrality 1939-45
London, Paladin 1985

Griffith, Richard

Fellow Travellers of the
Right - British Enthusiasts for Nazi
Germany
London, Constable 1980

Hünseler, Wolfgang	Das deutsche Kaiserreich und die irische Frage 1900-1914 Frankfurt, Peter Lang 1978
Inglis, Brian	Roger Casement London, Hodder & Stoughton 1973
Keating, Patrick	A Place amongst the Nations: Issues of Irish Foreign Policy Dublin, Institute of Public Administration 1978
Keogh, Dermot	Ireland and Europe 1919- 1989 Dublin and Cork, Hibernian University Press 1990
Keogh, Dermot	Twentieth Century Ireland: Nation and State Dublin, Gill & MacMillan 1994
Kluge, Hans-Dieter	Irland in der deutschen Geschichtswissenschaft, Politik und Propaganda vor 1914 und im ersten Weltkrieg Frankfurt, Lang 1985
Lee, Joseph	Ireland 1912-1985: Politics and Society Cambridge, Cambridge University Press 1989
Lerchenmüller, J.	Keltischer Sprengstoff: Kuno Meyer und die Geschichte der deutschen Keltologie PhD Dissertation Trinity College Dublin 1984
McGuinness, C. J.	Nomad: Memoirs of an Irish Sailor, Soldier, Pearl-fisher, Pirate, Gun-runner, Rum-runner, Rebel, Antarctic Explorer London, Methuen 1934

Manning, Maurice

The Blueshirts
Dublin, Gill & MacMillan
1987

O'Connor, P. J.

People Make Places - The
Story of the Irish Palatines
Newcastle, West/Limerick,
Oiracht na Mumhan Books 1989

O'Driscoll, Samuel N.M.
.

Irish-German Diplomatic
Relations 1922-39
MA Dissertation University
College Cork 1992

Oehlke, Andreas

Irland und die Iren in deutschen
Reisebeschreibungen des 18. und
19. Jahrhunderts
Frankfurt, Peter Lang 1991

O'Luing, Michael

Kuno Meyer 1858-1919: A
Biography
Dublin, Geogr. Publications 1991

O'Neill, Patrick

Ireland and Germany. A
Study in Literary Relations
New York, Lang 1985

Renzing, Rüdiger

Pfälzer in Irland.
Inst. für pfälzische Geschichte und
Volkskunde 1989

Sagarra, Eda

Frederick II and His Image
in Eighteenth-Century Dublin
In: Hermathena No 142,
1987, p. 50 - 58

Sagarra, Eda

Germanistik in Irland
The Scarlet Quarterly Nr 5,
1991, p. 42 - 44

Sawyer, Roger

Stephan, Enno

Sturm, Hubert

Wolff, Karin

Casement: The Flawed
Hero
London, Routledge & Kegan Paul
1984

Geheimauftrag Irland: Deutsche
Agenten im irischen Untergrund-
kampf 1939-1945
Hamburg, Gerhard Stalling 1961

Hakenkreuz und Kleeblatt:
Irland, die Alliierten und
das Dritte Reich 1933-1945
Frankfurt, Peter Lang 1984

Sir Roger Casement und
die Deutsch-Irischen Beziehungen
Berlin, Duncker & Humblot 1972

Acknowledgements

The author wishes to thank the following for permission to use the photographs in the centre of this book:

Sir Roger Casement:
The National Library of Ireland

Robert Smyllie and Col. Fritz Brase:
The Military Archives of Ireland

Francis Stuart:
Mrs Imogen Stuart

Commandant F.C. Sauerzweig
The Military Archives of Ireland

Commandant Fitzmaurice, Kapitän
Köhl, Baron von Hünefeld:
The Military Archives of Ireland

Professor Kuno Meyer:
The National Library of Ireland

Ernst Heinrich, Prince of Saxony:
Mrs Imogen Stuart

Dr. Georg von Dehn-Schmidt:
The German Embassy Dublin

Wilhelm von Kuhlmann:
The German Embassy Dublin

Dr. Eduard Hempel:
The German Embassy, Dublin

Dr. Hermann Katzenberger:
The German Embassy, Dublin